Police Crisis Intervention

(PGPS No. 80)

PERGAMON GENERAL PSYCHOLOGY SERIES

Editors: Arnold P. Goldstein, *Syracuse University*
Leonard Krasner, *SUNY, Stony Brook*

TITLES IN THE PERGAMON GENERAL PSYCHOLOGY SERIES
(Added Titles in Back of Volume)

The terms of our inspection copy service apply to all the above books. A complete catalogue of all books in the Pergamon International Library is available on request.

The Publisher will be pleased to receive suggestions for revised editions and new titles.

Police Crisis Intervention

By

Arnold P. Goldstein
Syracuse University

Philip J. Monti
Sergeant, Syracuse Police Department

Thomas J. Sardino
Chief, Syracuse Police Department

Donald J. Green
Deputy Chief, Syracuse Police Department

Pergamon Press

NEW YORK • OXFORD • TORONTO • SYDNEY • FRANKFURT • PARIS

Pergamon Press Offices:

U.S.A. Pergamon Press Inc., Maxwell House, Fairview Park, Elmsford, New York 10523, U.S.A.

U.K. Pergamon Press Ltd., Headington Hill Hall, Oxford OX3 0BW, England

CANADA Pergamon of Canada, Ltd., 150 Consumers Road, Willowdale, Ontario M2J, 1P9, Canada

AUSTRALIA Pergamon Press (Aust) Pty. Ltd., P O Box 544, Potts Point, NSW 2011, Australia

FRANCE Pergamon Press SARL, 24 rue des Ecoles, 75240 Paris, Cedex 05, France

FEDERAL REPUBLIC OF GERMANY Pergamon Press GmbH, 6242 Kronberg/Taunus, Pferdstrasse 1, Federal Republic of Germany

Library of Congress Cataloging in Publication Data:
  1. Police social work. 2. Crisis intervention (Psychiatry) I. Goldstein, Arnold P.
HV8079.2.P64   363.2'3   76-48283
ISBN 0-08-023873-4
ISBN 0-08-023874-2 pbk.

Printed in the United States of America

Contents

Contributors

Agnes Harrington

Police Officer
Syracuse Police Department

Joseph T. Himmelsbach

Chief, Special Evaluation Service
Hutchings Psychiatric Center, Syracuse, New York

Douglas L. Mace

Director, Education and Training
Syracuse Veterans Administration Hospital

William R. McPeak

Associate Professor
Syracuse University School of Social Work

Karen Sutton-Simon

Assistant Professor
Psychology Department, Oberlin College

Foreword

The need for timely resource material in police policies has never been greater than in the case of crisis intervention. I am especially pleased to see this book become available, because it provides information that is immediately useful to officers.

Crisis situations are unusually dangerous. They occur often, but in an unpredictable pattern. They tax an officer's skills to the limit, demanding tact, decisiveness, flexibility, and toughness, at a time when he or she is particularly vulnerable to personal harm.

The book does not waste the reader's time on generalities, but begins with a four-step action plan dealing with any crisis call. To make this advice even more specific, authoritative treatments of five common kinds of crises are then given. Another valuable feature of the book is a section on training methods which will be effective in presenting the skills to officers. Trainers are given detailed examples of exercises keyed to the intervention procedures.

The experience brought to this book by the authors is enhanced by a report of the Syracuse Police Department Program on Crisis Intervention Skill Training. This program combines classroom and field training, using techniques described in the book, followed by an evaluation of on-the-job results.

This book has wide potential as a ready-to-use training package. I hope that police executives, trainers, and above all, police officers answering crisis calls will take advantage of its value.

Chief Howard C. Shook
1st Vice President,
*   International Association of Chiefs of Police*
Chief of Police,
*   Middletown Township, Pennsylvania*
November, 1976

I

Police Intervention

Introduction

Crisis Intervention Manual for Police

1/ Introduction

PART I

Surveys completed in several police departments across the United States have revealed that only about 20% of the typical officer's time is spent identifying and apprehending criminals or in other law enforcement and crime control activities. Approximately 80% of the time the average officer is involved in service calls requiring primarily social regulation or what has been called *order maintenance*. The main concern of this book is with those order maintenance calls involving crisis intervention. These are calls involving family fights, mentally disturbed or intoxicated citizens, suicide attempts and victims of accidents, assault, rape or of other offenses. Such crisis calls have certain important similarities.

First, one or more highly emotional citizens are likely to be involved, though the particular emotion being expressed will vary according to the type of crisis. Aggressive feelings are usually the mark of family disputes. Anxiety or depression are typically present in suicide and accident crises. Rape and assault often lead to an hysterical and sometimes dazed victim response. And confusion and agitation are often the main features of mentally disturbed or intoxicated citizens.

Because of their highly emotional nature, a second similarity among most crisis calls is the high level of unpredictable danger, in the form of threats to the responding officer's safety. Family disputes and similar disturbance calls are particularly dangerous, accounting for 103 of the 786 police killed in the United States from 1963 to 1973. Forty percent of all police injuries also occur on these types of crisis intervention calls. The unpredictability of the sources of threat on these calls seems to be a major reason for their dangerous nature. It is one of the major purposes of this book to provide the police officer reader with appropriate information about crisis intervention procedures so that such danger will be minimized.

Calming an aggressive, confused, anxious or hysterical citizen is frequently a difficult task. Such persons must be calmed, not only for their own comfort and for that of others at the crisis scene, but also to permit the responding officer to get on with his job of resolving the crisis and restoring order. Thus, a second major purpose of this book is to instruct you, the reader, in a variety of procedures which have been used effectively to calm highly emotional individuals. Once the officer has calmed the individuals involved, and taken precautions to guard his own safety, he can begin to gather relevant information and to take appropriate police action. These procedures for effectively handling the steps in the crisis intervention process, i.e., information gathering and efforts to resolve the particular crisis, are also a special focus of the present book. In the chapter which follows, therefore, you will learn how to minimize threats to your safety, calm highly emotional citizens, gather, needed information from them under difficult circumstances, and take appropriate crisis-reducing action.

We are very much aware of the fact that crisis calls often place the responding officers in situations which not only may be dangerous, but also frustrating, unclear and unpleasant. Many officers feel that handling such calls is not "real" police work; and, furthermore, they often complain (with justification) that command personnel rarely reward success in this type of police activity. To those with such beliefs we can only state our own view that the effective resolvers of human crises provide an extremely important service, one often not available from others for the citizen in crisis. Theirs is a service which may not always be recognized by their police force superiors, but is, nevertheless, exceedingly well appreciated by the persons they serve. The officer who successfully intervenes in a family dispute; who restores calm to an agitated assault victim; who correctly refers an irate tenant to the proper agency; who effectively handles the intoxicated, drugged, mentally disturbed or suicidal citizen, has very much to be proud of indeed. He or she is, in our view, an especially good example of what the modern police officer should be.

PART II

To aid you in developing your own crisis intervention skills, we have gone beyond the description of specific crisis intervention procedures in this book (see Chapter 2). The effective officer must possess not only well-developed intervention skills, but also in-depth understanding of specific types of crises, what causes them, how people tend to react to them, and how the nature of each crisis is likely to affect the success or failure of your efforts to resolve it. Therefore, we also provide a series of chapters dealing in detail with specific types of crises. Each is written by an individual with many years of professional expertise in dealing with persons in the particular type of crisis discussed. Thus, we hope to provide you with the knowledge and views of skilled professionals with relevant, first-hand crisis intervention experience.

McPeak, in Chapter 3, examines family disputes. He describes normal and abnormal families; how members of a family can successfully communicate, or fail to communicate; various types of family crises; violence and conflict in families; and then offers several very practical suggestions for police officers who may have to intervene in such crises.

In Chapter 4, Himmelsbach focuses on the mentally ill individual. He examines causes and types of mental illness, placing particular attention on signs and symptoms of various mental disturbances, in order to help the responding officer both recognize and interpret the meaning and significance of such states as anxiety, confusion and suspiciousness, when they occur. As in all the other chapters in this part of the book, the author makes a special point to provide suggested crisis intervention procedures. In this case, Himmelsbach instructs us in special problems and intervention procedures for paranoid, delusional, catatonic, withdrawn and highly aggressive individuals.

A great many crisis calls are directly or indirectly caused by alcohol or drug abuse, the topic of Chapter 5. In this chapter, Mace provides us with relevant abuse figures and facts; describes various types of drug substances; helps us understand the difference between use, misuse, dependency and addiction; presents his views favoring decriminalization of marijuana possession; describes different types of drug abusers; highlights drug-associated crises; and gives a number of recommendations for effective police response to these crises.

Harrington and Sutton-Simon, in the next chapter, instruct us about crisis situations associated with the crime of rape. They provide us with relevant information, and seek to dispel a number of the myths associated with the topic. They describe rape much more as a crime of violence, than as a sexual crime; offer a profile of the rapist and the typical rape victim; and, in particular, stress useful police procedures in assisting the victim and in conducting a proper and efficient investigation.

In the final chapter in this part, Himmelsbach explores crisis and crisis intervention with suicidal individuals. Among other elements, he examines why people may seek to kill themselves; who such people are likely to be; and the different methods different types of people use. Particularly valuable is the author's discussion of how to determine the actual risk of a suicide attempt on such calls. Further, Himmelsbach tells us about a number of highly useful steps which responding officers may take in protecting their own safety on such calls; in establishing initial contact with the citizen; and in conducting a conversation with such persons which may lower the risk of successful suicide. He also discusses how and when force should be used, and gives a number of suggestions for appropriate police response to both successful and unsuccessful suicide attempts.

Part II of this book, therefore, is a detailed examination of five types of crises: family disputes, mental disturbance, drug and alcohol intoxication, rape and suicide. The crisis intervention procedures presented throughout these chapters, hopefully, will prove useful to responding police officers not only in these five, common crisis situations, but also on other types of crisis calls involving threats to officer safety, highly emotional citizens and the other characteristics of crisis examined in this book. We urge you, therefore, to also try to apply the lessons and procedures of these chapters, when and where you feel they may prove useful: when dealing with assault and accident victims, in responding to a "lost child" call, when handling a frightened runaway, in interviewing a burglary victim and in the host of other similar situations which make up your daily routine.

PART III

Part III of this book is written for the police trainer. Most readers will be able to learn the information in the bulk of the chapters which follow simply by reading them. But, it is often true that material you learn by reading, through lectures, or by other passive means alone is often not learned well enough for you to apply it effectively on a continuing basis where it counts — on patrol, in the field, on the job. For new learning to transfer from the pages of a book to patrol application, in most cases, the learner must actively participate in the learning situation.

The two chapters which make up Part III concern just such an active, involving, learning process, a process we call "Structured Learning Training." In this training approach, a series of behavioral skills which constitute effective crisis intervention are demonstrated to small groups of police trainees. They are given structured opportunities to rehearse these skills, provided with feedback about the quality of their rehearsals, and helped to take part in these activities in such a way that the chances are good that what they learn will actually be used on patrol.

Chapter 8 describes the background and development of "Structured Learning Training," and Chapter 9 is a step-by-step trainer's guide for its use in teaching crisis intervention skills. We also provide, in this last chapter, research evidence which demonstrates the effectiveness of this training approach in developing such skills. Since our research results are clearly positive, we would urge that, whenever possible, interested police departments and similar agencies make use of this means for crisis intervention instruction.

We wish to close this introductory chapter by reaffirming our belief that the skilled, effective, professional police officer is one who is highly competent in his or her ability to intervene successfully in a variety of human crises. The chapters which follow are dedicated to this goal.

2/ Crisis Intervention Manual for Police

We have devoted Chapter 2 to describing specific procedures which responding police may use to effectively deal with crisis situations. As we discussed in the preceding chapter, police crisis intervention often involves unexpected threats to the officer's physical safety. We will focus on this problem in the first section of the chapter, as a means of giving you information which may help you to better predict such threats to your safety; better prepare you in procedures for spotting potential sources of danger; and thus, hopefully, reduce the possibility of injury or death resulting from your crisis intervention activities.

Once you have taken initial steps to protect your safety, you are faced with the task of dealing effectively with the crisis situation. To do so, your next job will be to calm the highly emotional citizens involved in the crisis. In the second section of this chapter we will provide you with several procedures for quieting highly emotional citizens, and also offer guidelines to help you decide which calming procedures to use with which types of citizens.

After quieting the scene, you will be able to proceed to gather the information you need in order to decide upon and take appropriate action. Thus, in our third section we will describe several information gathering procedures and, again, emphasize that different procedures will best be used with different citizens. In the final section we will outline several courses of action you may choose to take in order to resolve the crisis situation.

Thus, proceeding in order of occurrence, this chapter provides you with very specific information to aid you in dealing effectively with crisis intervention calls by describing procedures for:

1. Observing and protecting against threats to your safety.
2. Calming the crisis situation.
3. Gathering relevant information.
4. Taking appropriate action.

We urge you to learn these procedures well. They will help protect your safety.

Road experience, of course, is a key ingredient in any officer's learning to perform in a manner which keeps threats to his or her safety as low as possible. But don't depend on road experience alone. The majority of the 103 officers killed on such calls had five or more years of road experience! These procedures will help you handle the crisis call in an effective and *flexible* manner. We stress "flexible" because no single procedure will work well in all, or usually even most, crisis situations. To be truly effective, you will have to:

1. Develop skill in using several crisis intervention procedures.
2. Know when to employ each procedure.

Finally, your effective use of these crisis interventions will also reduce callbacks, increase community goodwill toward your police department, and add to your own sense of competence and professionalism.

OBSERVING AND PROTECTING
AGAINST THREATS TO YOUR SAFETY

Because the citizens involved are often overexcited and highly emotional, and you can't predict the threats to your safety at the time, crisis intervention is very dangerous police business. As we noted earlier, crisis intervention disturbance calls are a major source of police deaths and injuries. They must be handled with great care, and must be seen as anything but "routine." Your safety, your health, and your life may depend on it.

Since the most gentle-appearing citizens can become abusive

under certain circumstances; since the most harmless-appearing objects can be used as weapons; and since no officer can prevent all threats to his or her safety and still function effectively, there will always remain some danger in your handling of crisis calls. But such danger can be reduced substantially. And, you yourself can take these steps. It has been shown that threats to your safety will be reduced if you are adequately prepared *in advance* for the crisis situation in which you are intervening. After radio dispatch, but while still in your patrol car on the way to the crisis scene, you should:

1. Consider your prior experience on similar calls.
2. Anticipate that the unexpected may actually happen.
3. Form a tentative plan of action.

We urge you, first of all, to consider your prior experience on similar calls so you can recall and review *all* the relevant past events that you have actually been involved in. You should think over not only how crises of the same type as the present call *usually* unfold, and how you *usually* have handled them, but also recall and review *unusual* past calls of this type. They may occur again this way, and if you are prepared, your safety is increased. Rehearse in your imagination the various ways (usual and unusual) in which crises like these have developed, and, specifically, what you will do in each instance. As you think through these several alternatives, place particular emphasis on threats to your safety. What objects have been used against you as weapons in the past? What types of people have abused or attacked you when you didn't expect it? What did you fail to observe, scan, do, or have someone else do which put you in danger in the past?

Once you have *thoroughly* reviewed your past experience on similar calls, and used it in this way to increase your preparedness, we urge you to imagine threats to your safety which might occur even though they never have before. That is, anticipate that the unexpected might actually happen. Remember, the policeman's enemy is the false security caused by routine. A salesman can approach 50 customers the same way. Forty-nine make a purchase, the fiftieth refuses. Since the salesman is so generally effective, he ignores this fiftieth customer and goes on using the same approach in the future. A police officer doesn't have the same luxury. His handling of forty-nine family fight calls can all proceed well, and cause no physical harm to the officer. If the officer is not wary on the fiftieth, not alert and prepared for both expected and unexpected dangers, he may lose not a sale, but his life.

It is a hard task to get "psyched up" call after call, but each is a real or potential threat to your safety. You must thoroughly review the possible dangers before proceeding — both those that have actually happened to you on earlier calls, and those you imagine could happen.

Preparing through rehearsal will be even more effective if you are thoroughly familiar with your patrol area and the people who reside in it. Knowing who does or does not belong in a given residence, who works in a certain store, or how to get in and out of a given business establishment may prove to be very valuable safety information if you have to intervene in a crisis at one of these places. Clearly, therefore, it is worth your effort to get to know the people and places which make up your patrol area *before* need arises.

With all that you must do to just drive safely but quickly to the crisis scene in this short time, you have a lot occupying your thinking already. We have tried to make you even busier by what we described above as rehearsal, in your imagination, of the scene, the crisis, and the threats to your safety which may develop. There is one final aspect of your in-the-car responsibility to your own safety which we wish to discuss. The emphasis up to this point has been on what the *citizen* may do to you, and how you might prepare yourself to respond. But only part of the danger to responding officers is citizen-caused. Serious injury or death may result from events or chains of behaviors which *officers* begin. You may, in other words, sometimes be a serious threat to your own safety.

Most of our emphasis thus far has been on the dangers of being unprepared when responding to crisis intervention calls. An equally serious problem (to his own safety) is often the officer who is *too* prepared. Notice that earlier we described the final preparation step (in the car) as "form a *tentative* plan of action." We stressed "tentative" because although being prepared is very desirable, the officer who is "sure" in his own mind about what will happen can often *cause* it to happen. This is sometimes called a "self-fulfilling prophecy."

The officer who, after considering all past experiences and all possible relevant crises, decides that the citizens at the crisis scene are certain to attack him, may approach them in such a hostile or aggressive way that he may provoke the very attack he was expecting. Be prepared, but be open to the possibility that what you have decided *probably* will happen still has some chance of not happening. Form a tentative plan of action, and begin acting on it, but don't finalize it until you observe the actual crisis and gather all relevant information. A tenth repeat call to a family having a dispute (which on the nine earlier times ended with the disputants quieting down) may unexpectedly turn violent and cause you serious injury.

Remember, the steps to follow on the way to a crisis call are:

1. Consider your prior experience on similar calls.
2. Anticipate that the unexpected may actually happen.
3. Form a tentative plan of action.

CALMING THE SITUATION

Step 1. Observe and Neutralize Threats to Your Safety

You have now arrived at the scene of the crisis call. If you have done a good job of preparing on the way, you arrive with both a tentative plan in mind, and some specific ideas about threats to your safety which may be present. Your first step on arrival, therefore, should be to *observe and neutralize possible threats to your safety*. By this we mean not only removing the obvious weapons such as guns and knives, but also removing or neutralizing the heavy and throwable objects (ashtrays, folding chairs, etc.), scissors, kitchen utensils, boiling water (in a pot on the stove, or in a coffee cup), and the like. We would also recommend routinely and immediately separating disputants; placing yourself away from windows and staircases; avoiding turning your back on any of the disputants; and, both knowing where your partner is, and, if possible, actually having him in view — even when each of you is with a different disputant in a different room.

You should also take what steps you can to minimize threats to your safety which are caused by things *you* do or fail to do. At times it may be best to cruise past the crisis scene and quickly scan the places and people before returning there to park. If the disturbance call is in progress, do not park your car immediately in front of the location of the crisis. While parking away from the scene may make you harder to find by other responding personnel, and also make it a bit harder for you to get to your radio and equipment, these disadvantages are outweighed by the one main advantage of such parking — the disputants won't see you arrive.On all types of disturbance calls, you increase your safety if you surprise the disputants, rather than having them see you first and possibly prepare to attack you.

Wherever you park, position your car so that it won't get boxed in. Secure your car, so that it is difficult for anyone not authorized by you to get at your equipment, or anything else in the car which may be used as a weapon. A secure car will also increase the chances that you will have radio access to assistance if you need it. As you arrive, and while you're still in the car, look over the crisis scene for anything you can learn about the nature and scope of the disturbance. Bicycles on a lawn, people sitting or standing on a porch, a car with its motor running, the number of rooms in the house with lights on, and the general noise level are among the many things you may observe which can give you clues to how many people are at the crisis scene, their ages and their possible emotional states.

Approach the scene quietly, and separately from your partner, if you have one. Do not stand directly in front of the door, as someone may shoot through it; or, as has happened with glass doors, throw something through it. Stand to the side of the doorway, and, if it is a door which opens *toward* you, be sure to stand to the side away from the hinges so that the door can't be pushed into you. Be ready to scan the room inside for threats to your safety as soon as the door is opened. Be prepared to enter. but be sure not to place your arm, leg or nightstick into a partially opened door space as the door may be quickly shut on you, thus holding you almost defenseless.

Upon entering the apartment or house, visually "frisk" everyone. Determine who is in the apartment and where they are. Get and keep everyone in sight. Look for and remove all actual or potential weapons. See that disputants are separated; and be sure that you avoid standing in places in which you are vulnerable to attack or injury. In carrying out these steps, remember that it is not only an adult male who may attack you. Adult females, the elderly, and adolescents may all possess weapons, or may otherwise initiate aggressive behavior toward you. While using these methods to neutralize threats to your safety, do not overlook your own gun. A high percentage of the 103 officers mentioned earlier who were killed on disturbance calls, were murdered by their own service revolvers.

Finally, unless you must physically restrain a citizen, try to avoid crowding, threatening, grabbing or otherwise touching an already hostile person, as it may provoke him to even more violent behavior. At times you will be able to be aware enough of someone's non-verbal behavior to spot violence just before it occurs, i.e., after the fuse is lit, but before the explosion. Signs of impending violence often include a crouched torso, clenched fists, grinding teeth, dilated pupils, flared nostrils, flushed cheeks.

Step 2. Create a First Impression of Non-Hostile Authority

Once you feel you have made a good beginning at protecting your own physical safety and the safety of the citizens involved, you may move to the second step in calming the situation. Keep in mind, however, that you may be threatened with danger at any time during the crisis call, so remain on guard for unpredicted violence throughout *all* phases of the call. The second step in calming the situation is to *create a first impression of non-hostile authority.*

How someone reacts to you will, of course, be determined by his personality, his history with other police officers, and, by the crisis itself. But your behavior, especially your first impression behavior, will have a lot to do with how aggressively the citizen behaves and how cooperative he is with your efforts to calm the situation and resolve the crisis. Therefore, in the initial phases of your dealing with the person in crisis, we recommend that you behave as a non-hostile authority by taking charge and instructing that person in what you want him to do, in a firm, fair, even and direct manner.

In doing so, it is important to avoid being either too soft or too harsh. The officer who too gently asks the individual to do such and such will often fail to achieve his purpose because he's neither gotten the person's attention to a sufficient degree, nor made the citizen feel sufficiently secure or reassured by his presence. The officer who opens his arrival at a crisis call by being too harsh, by leaning too hard on the people involved, may also fail to achieve his purposes of calming the scene and resolving the crisis. In fact, just the opposite may occur. The disturbance level may actually increase, and threats to the officer's safety may actually become more possible.

Step 3. Calm the Emotional Citizen

Whether they are directly involved or just observers, the people at a crisis scene are quite likely to be in a highly emotional state. Which particular emotion is being shown will depend partly on the citizen and partly on the nature of the crisis (family fight, rape, accident, attempted suicide, assault, burglary or an episode of mental disturbance or intoxication). However, regardless of whether the persons involved are highly aggressive, anxious, confused, or hysterical, it is the officer's job to first *calm the emotional citizen* before he will be able to gather the information he needs to carry out proper police procedure, and bring the crisis to an appropriate conclusion.

We have stressed elsewhere that the effective police officer is a *flexible* officer. He does not try to use a single approach in all situations but, instead, varies his behavior depending upon the citizen and the nature of the crisis. In order to be flexible, he must know a variety of approaches well, and develop (with experience) the knowledge of which one to apply at which times. The material which follows is a brief description of the several procedures which effective officers have actually used successfully to calm citizen emotions in crisis situations.

Show understanding. By your words, tone of voice, facial expression and gestures, you can make it clear to the citizen that you accurately understand *what* the person is feeling and *how strongly* he is feeling it. For example: "You're really feeling very angry and upset at him." Or, "It can be awfully frightening when something like this happens." Or, "I understand that you're feeling very sad and alone after a loss like this." Note that in these examples and in the calming methods discussed below, an officer remains impartial and maintains his professional role by avoiding taking sides. He says, "You're really feeling very angry and upset at him." and not, "You've got every right to feel angry and upset at him."

Model. By your words, tone of voice, facial expression and gestures, you can make it clear to the person that you, the officer, are responding calmly to the crisis situation. Your calmness and appearance of control can serve as a model. By removing your hat, sitting down, speaking at a normal conversational rate and level, you communicate that *you* feel no need to be upset, angry or anxious. Since we all are often ready to imitate people in authority, a demonstration of calmness by an officer will frequently have a calming effect on highly emotional people.

Reassure. In using modeling to calm the situation, the officer's own behavior serves as an example which we hope the person will imitate. Using reassurance aids in a further way because the officer not only behaves in a calm manner, but, in addition, gives the citizen reasons why he too should feel calmer. For example, you can reassure with such sentences as: "It will be O.K.." "I've handled many like this." "The ambulance will be here very soon." "The doctor will know how to handle this." "We've got him under control." Reassurance will work particularly well in calming a situation if the officer has done a good initial job of establishing a first impression of himself as a non-hostile, authority figure.

Encourage talking. It is very difficult for someone to continue yelling, screaming, crying, fighting or behaving in a highly emotional manner while at the same time trying to answer a series of questions. Thus, encouraging the person to talk is often an effective means for calming him down. Sometimes it will prove useful to encourage talking about the crisis itself. (Encourage talking: Ventilation.) Here, the officer asks the person to begin at the beginning; asks numerous questions regarding exactly who did what, where, in what sequence, and at what time; includes several open-ended questions; and takes notes at a deliberate pace in order to slow down the citizen's rate of talking.

Some people, however, will remain upset when encouraged to talk about the crisis because they are now being asked to describe the very situation which upset them in the first place. When this occurs, or as a substitute procedure, it is often useful to encourage people to talk about matters other than the crisis. (Encourage talking: Diversion.) In essence, this procedure is an attempt to divert their attention away from the crisis and their feelings about it. Here the officer seeks "background information" which he claims he needs for his formal report, such as the names of the people involved, their addresses, ages, phone numbers, occupations, legal relationship and so forth. (See Appendix II.)

Use distraction. At times, an effective means for calming emotional citizens will be to divert their attention from the crisis in ways other than by asking for background information. Distraction procedures are likely to have a rather temporary effect, however. Thus, you must be prepared to follow them with the use of other calming procedures if necessary. Distraction may be accomplished by:

1. Asking a favor, e.g., "May I have a glass of water?"
2. Asking a question totally irrelevant to the situation, e.g., "Can you tell me where you got that (household item)?"
3. Asking a question relevant to the crisis situation, but opposite to what the citizen is likely to expect, e.g., "Would you really prefer to be arrested?"
4. Offering an observation totally irrelevant to the crisis situation, e.g., "I've got the same brand of T.V., but we've been having trouble with it lately."
5. Giving a suggestion or command which tells the citizen to continue exactly what he expects you to try to stop, e.g., "Please yell louder."

Use humor. There will be citizens with whom you may effectively use humor as a calming procedure. Humor can put the crisis in a more accurate and less serious perspective; it can communicate to the citizen that you are not overly upset by what is happening (modeling); and, it can often cool tempers in a crisis of a highly aggressive nature.

The first six methods we have presented for calming crisis situations, may all be considered "conversational" methods. By showing understanding, modeling, reassuring, encouraging talking, or using distraction or humor, the officer seeks to calm the emotional citizen by words and deeds designed to have a quieting effect. We recommend that one or more of these first six calming methods be used initially in crisis situations unless, of course, physical dangers to yourself or to other citizens are apparent. When these conversational methods fail, we recommend use (in the order presented below) of two "assertive" methods for calming citizens in crisis.

Repeat and outshout. When individuals are very angry, very anxious, very depressed or very confused, they are tuned into their own feelings, but often are unresponsive and even unaware of the feelings, communications and, sometimes, even presence of others. The officer may have to repeat himself several times to "get through" to the citizen. When the emotion is anger and an altercation is still in progress, you may have to outshout the citizen to be heard. This display of authority, or similar steps such as slamming a clipboard loudly, and so forth, will often yield an immediate quieting effect.

Use physical restraint. When conversational calming methods fail, when repetition and outshouting prove not to be assertive enough, or where considerations of physical danger demand it, the officer must physically restrain and subdue the highly aggressive citizen. You are urged to use just enough force to accomplish this goal, and to avoid using excessive force. While subduing one disputant, remain aware of the other one. In family disputes, for example, it is not unusual for a complainant wife to turn on the officer and try to resist her husband's arrest even though she was the one who called the police in the first place.

There will be crises in which calming the citizen is best handled by means other than the conversational or assertive methods described above.

Use trusted others. Circumstances may occur in crisis situations which make it appropriate for the officer to ask someone else to either assist in, or take full responsibility for calming the emotional citizen. This "someone else" may be a fellow officer, but often will be a trusted friend, relative or neighbor of the emotional citizen. Using trusted others as calming sources may prove necessary when you are too busy with danger or threat aspects of the crisis; when there are too many highly emotional citizens involved in the crisis for you to handle alone (or with your partner); when the citizen is too fearful of police; when the citizen speaks only a foreign language; and when conversational and assertive methods have not succeeded.

Temporarily ignore. We have described a number of calming procedures and suggested some broad guidelines for the rough order in which they ought to be used. There are times, however, when the effective officer will use none of these procedures but decide instead to deal with the emotional citizen by temporarily ignoring him. Depending upon threats to officer or citizen safety, and upon emergency aspects of the crisis itself, the officer may have to devote priority attention to matters other than the citizen's feelings. The bleeding auto accident victim must be given first aid while her hysterical spouse's behavior is ignored for the time being. The disputants in a barroom disturbance must be separated and restrained before you can attend to the distress of the bar's owner. And burglarized premises may have to be secured before you can listen to the anxious and upset tenant.

We have presented several alternative methods for calming the anger, anxiety, hysteria or confusion of highly emotional citizens in crisis situations. While we have provided a general idea regarding the order in which we recommend these procedures be used, it is not possible to provide you with more specific rules for matching procedures to specific emotions or specific crises. For one officer, modeling may be very effective in calming participants in certain family fights in some cases. In other such fights the officer may have to resort to physical restraint. Another officer may be excellent at reassuring accident victims, while a third may be more effective with other techniques in similar crises.

Which procedures in which crises, with which citizens, will work most effectively for *you* is a matter you will have to determine from your own experience. This chapter simply asks that you not expect one or two procedures to work in all situations, and that you try to be flexible and work out *your* best match by trying different calming procedures with different types of crises and citizens.

Remember, the steps for **Calming the Situation** are:

1. **Observe and neutralize threats to your safety.**
2. **Create a first impression of non-hostile authority.**
3. **Calm the emotional citizen.**

GATHERING RELEVANT INFORMATION

Step 1. Explain to the Citizen What You Want Him to Discuss with You and Why

You have calmed the crisis situation so that the people involved will be more accurate and reliable sources for the information you need in order to take appropriate action.[1] Your information gathering, of course, began with your radio call and was supplemented by observing the people and events as you tried to calm the situation. Now that everyone is relatively calmer, your main information gathering activity must begin. The first step in doing so is to *explain to the citizen what you want him to discuss with you and why.* You should carefully explain in detail the purpose of the interview you are about to conduct so that the person knows the types of information you expect,[2] and is willing to cooperate with you in providing it. Once the stage is correctly set (that is, once you have successfully begun to calm the citizen, told him what to expect from the interview, and gained his cooperation), you can begin the interview.

Step 2. Interview the Citizen so as to Gain Details of the Crisis as Clearly as Possible

While it is obviously true that the main purpose of the officer's interview at a crisis scene is to gather relevant information, we wish to briefly mention two other important goals which may be accomplished at the same time. If you conduct the interview in a highly professional manner, providing the citizens with an impression of a skilled, aware, sensitive and purposeful interviewer, you will not only obtain maximal amounts of accurate information, but will also *give* information about yourself and your skills which will:

1. maintain the level of emotional calm you built earlier, and
2. build goodwill for yourself and the police department you represent.

In our earlier discussion of Calming the Situation, we mentioned several procedures and explained that the choice of one over the other would depend on the situation, i.e., the particular citizen involved, and the nature and level of his emotional state. In general, we recommended that you use first one or more of the conversational calming methods and then, if necessary, shift to more assertive procedures. We wish to make a number of similar recommendations about the several interviewing procedures we will describe.

As was true of calming procedures, different interviewing methods are best used for different citizens. You will have to decide which

---

[1] In many crisis calls you will be able to successfully calm the people involved, and gather the relevant information you're seeking. In many other crises, however, you'll have to use calming procedures throughout the entire call. In still other cases, the procedures may have to be continued still further by a neighbor or relative after you leave.

[2] See the Family Crisis Intervention Report (Appendix II). It indicates the type of information you may need to obtain when responding to family dispute calls.

ones to use, and when, based on your own experiences in crisis situations. We can, however, provide general guidelines.

We have described three sets of interviewing procedures below. The procedures are presented in order of increasing directiveness on the part of the interviewer (officer). Thus, Open-ended questions and Listening (procedures 1 and 2) require much less directiveness and assertiveness than, for example, Confrontation and Demanding (procedures 9 and 10). In general, we recommend that you begin your interview with the least directive procedures, and become increasingly directive only as circumstances warrant. While low directiveness procedures will be all that prove necessary in many crisis situations, the very angry, very anxious or highly confused citizen will require forceful interview procedures before you can obtain accurate information from him. The specific procedures for interviewing citizens in crisis are:

Non-Directive Procedures
    1. Open-ended questions
    2. Listening
    3. Closed-ended questions
    4. Restatement of content (paraphrasing)
    5. Reflection of feeling

Moderately-Directive Procedures
    6. Selective inattention and use of silence
    7. Encouragement and use of specific and simplified invitations
    8. Self-disclosure and use of immediacy

Highly-Directive Procedures
    9. Confrontation
    10. Demanding

We now wish to describe each of these procedures in greater detail.

Open-ended questions. Questions which give the citizen the freedom and opportunity to give an answer of considerable length, an answer shaped mostly by the citizen's wishes and not the officer's, are open-ended questions. Examples of such questions in a crisis context include: "What happened here?" "What do you mean by nagging?" "Why do you describe him as crazy?" These are usually questions which begin with "what," "why" or "how."

Listening. How well the citizen feels the officer is listening to him will clearly influence how open and detailed his statement will be. You can communicate the fact that you are listening both by what you do and what you avoid doing. The skilled listener maintains eye contact, shows by his posture and gestures that he is paying attention, and makes occasional comments to the citizen which also show interest and attention, e.g., "I see what you mean." "I can understand that." The skilled listener also avoids trying to interview more than one person at a time, remembers to reuse calming procedures as often as necessary, and physically separates disputants so that they will not distract one another.

Closed-ended questions. Questions which can be answered with yes or no, or with brief, factual replies are closed-ended questions. They are questions which usually begin with "do," "is" or "are." Such questions are a necessary and valuable part of your interview, and only present a problem when used where open-ended questions would be preferable. That is, closed-ended questions may be inefficient (when you have to ask a great many of them instead of a few open-ended questions), or leading (when they suggest answers to the citizen, a fault usually less true of open-ended questions).

Restatement of content (paraphrasing). Using this procedure serves to show the citizen you are "with him" and, thus, are paying attention; and also encourages him to go on and provide further details. The procedure consists of saying back to the citizen, in words somewhat different than his own if possible (i.e., paraphrasing), the essence of what he has already said to you. Examples of restating content include: "So you want your husband home tonight even though he hit you." "You're saying you did everything you were supposed to: paid the rent, didn't make too much noise, and so on."

You will find that perhaps your most effective use of restatement of content, as far as getting the citizen to provide you with more details on a given topic, will involve restating a single word, the word most central to the topic you want elaborated by the citizen. Such words, often presented as a one word question, include "Fight?" after a citizen states: "We fight every day." and you wish to learn more about their past; "Never?" after the same complainant spouse states: "He's never been a good husband." and you'd like to know more about any positive strengths in their relationship; and "Hopeless?" when you wish to learn about any optimistic thoughts after an attempted suicide in which the citizen describes his world as "all black, hopeless and terrible."

Reflection of feeling. Whereas restating content stresses saying back to the citizen one or more of the *facts* in his statement, this procedure focuses on expressing to the citizen an understanding of his main *feelings.* To reflect a citizen's feelings accurately, you must pay attention both to what the citizen is saying and to how he is saying it. The complainant spouse noted above, who tells you, "We fight every day. He's never been a good husband." might be told, "You really seem to feel very angry at him, and not very hopeful things will change." The suicidal citizen might have his feelings reflected with an officer statement such as, "Everything seems just awful to you, nothing's even slightly hopeful." The point about reflection of feeling is that when people feel that you understand their apparent or even somewhat hidden feelings, they are much more likely to continue to provide you with information.

Selective inattention and use of silence. An excited citizen will often provide the officer with details which are either irrelevant to what you need in order to take appropriate action or, if relevant, in excess of what you need. That is, in contrast to the reluctant, resistive or too silent citizen, you may be faced with a disputant, a victim or a relative who talks too much, and who is difficult to divert back to the task at hand. Simply failing to pay attention to irrelevant or excessive statements will often be an effective means of stemming the flow. Thus, in a manner opposite to our earlier listening instructions, here you should respond to unwanted and excessive statements by *not* maintaining eye contact, *not* providing posture and gestures which signify paying attention, and *not* making statements which show understanding.

Encouragement and use of specific and simplified invitations. People under stress often become quite confused and disorganized in their thinking and speech. Simple questions like "What happened here?" may yield agitated and erroneous answers from such individuals. Under these circumstances it will be your task to simplify matters for the citizen, and make questioning very concrete and stepwise. "Encouragement and use of specific and simplified invitations" means you must often be a patient questioner, restater or reflector who sets up and asks a simplified series of questions; who praises the citizen not only for answers but even for trying to answer; who asks only one question at a time; and who builds your interview with one question or statement logically following the other. In this manner, especially when combined with appropriate calming techniques, the individual is likely to become less confused and agitated and more accurate and detailed in his statement.

Self-disclosure and use of immediacy. People tend to be more open with those who are open with them. We tend to be more disclosing about our own thoughts, feelings, ideas and backgrounds when others first reveal such information to us. There will be crisis situations in which self-disclosure by the responding officer will prove to be a useful interviewing procedure. We wish to stress, however, that there is an important difference between private self-disclosure and public self-disclosure.

Private self-disclosure would include information about any fighting or arguing the officer has done with his own wife, any feelings of depression the officer himself has experienced, any fears the officer has about being assaulted. Such private self-disclosure is *not* a useful or appropriate interviewing procedure. It will tend to diminish the officer in the eyes of the citizen, and fail to increase citizen self-disclosure. Public self-disclosure, in contrast, does involve the officer revealing information about himself; but not what we have described above as private information. Thus, the self-disclosing officer may usefully reveal *public* experiences he has had which are relevant to the crisis interview, places he has been, types of people he has dealt with, and the like.

This moderately directive interview procedure also involves "use of immediacy." This term refers to the effects of positive officer comments about the immediate officer-citizen relationship on further disclosure by the citizen. Comments by the officer such as, "I can see just from what you've said so far that you're really trying hard." or "You make me feel you can be trusted, so maybe you impress other people the same way." are examples of use of immediacy. As we cautioned earlier, remember to avoid the appearance of taking sides when making statements like these.

Confrontation. Confrontation, as an interviewing procedure, involves pointing out to a citizen any discrepancies between either a) two things he has said, or b) something he has said and the quite different way in which he has said it. An example of the first, a content-content discrepancy, would be, "You said he started it all, but you also said what sounded like he was just minding his own business when you went over to him." The second, a content-feeling discrepancy, is illustrated by, "You told me you want him out of here tonight and you don't care how, but now you're really getting angry at me for arresting him."

Demanding. The several methods described to this point may all prove unsuccessful if the citizen is very hostile, resistive or indifferent to your interviewing efforts. Both non-directive and moderately-directive procedures may simply not work for some citizens, and greater interviewer directiveness may be required. It is here that the officer's earlier success in creating a first impression of non-hostile authority will pay off. Demanding requires that you firmly instruct the citizen about what he is to tell you, and tell you now! It is a no-nonsense, business-like (but not hostile) stand by the interviewing officer, one in which the officer insists, rather than asks; tells rather than requests.

The resistant citizen. There will be citizens you will meet on crisis calls who, in spite of your skilled use of the interviewing procedures described above — including "demanding" — remain reluctant or resistant to giving you the information you need to form a sound plan of action. They may be too angry, too frightened or too confused. When this occurs, we suggest that you once again make use of one or more of the procedures described earlier in this manual for calming the highly emotional citizen. Specifically, the reluctant or resistant citizen is likely to become a more cooperative interviewer if the officer:

1. Shows understanding
2. Provides reassurance
3. Offers encouragement
4. Patiently repeats
5. Uses humor

In addition to using these calming procedures, a number of officers have effectively reduced citizen resistance to providing information by:

1. Restating their questions in a briefer and clearer manner.
2. Praising the citizen, and showing appreciation for whatever partial or incomplete information the citizen has revealed.
3. Carefully prompting the citizen to provide answers by, in a sense, giving him several possible answers from which to choose.[3]

Step 3. Show That You Understand the Citizen's Statements and Give Accurate Answers to His Questions

The person being interviewed will be most likely to continue providing the information you are seeking, if you show that person, in a variety of ways, that he is understood. These include certain of the methods described earlier: restatement of content, reflection of feeling, direct statements to the citizen, e.g., "I understand what you mean." and other officer statements which show the citizen you are "staying with him." Giving clear, patient and accurate answers to citizen questions will also make your eventual task of taking appropriate action easier, as the informed citizen is more likely to be a cooperative source in deciding upon and carrying out crisis-resolving solutions.

Step 4. Revise Your Plan of Action if Appropriate

Recall that the effective officer forms a tentative plan of action while still in his patrol car, on his way to the crisis scene. His observations at that scene, the events which occur as he calms the citizens, and the facts and impressions he gathers from interviewing them, all provide him with information necessary to revise his plan and finalize it so that he can act upon it. By "finalize" it, we mean:

1. Decide in his own thinking that the plan is a wise one

---

[3] In using prompting procedures, the officer must be careful to avoid self-fulfilling prophecies. That is, he should give the citizen as complete a range of answers as possible to choose from. Otherwise, he runs the serious risk of putting "words in the citizen's mouth," and, thus, getting answers which merely serve to fulfill the officer's expectations, not provide accurate information about the crisis.

2. Check it out with his partner, if possible
3. Plan on how to present it to the people involved.

In summary, in **Gathering Relevant Information**, you should:

1. **Explain to the citizen what you want him to discuss with you and why.**
2. **Interview the citizen so as to get details of the crisis as clearly as possible.**
3. **Show that you understand the citizen's statements and give accurate answers to his questions.**
4. **Revise your plan of action if appropriate.**

TAKING APPROPRIATE ACTION

You have quieted the people involved in the crisis call, and obtained the information you need to decide upon and begin taking appropriate action. The steps we recommend that you follow in taking appropriate action are:

Step 1. Carefully explain your plan of action to the people involved.
Step 2. Check that they understand and agree with your plan of action.
Step 3. Carry out your plan of action.

Steps 1 and 2 seem to require no further explanation. Step 3, however, can take many forms and, thus, will be the main topic of this section. We emphasized earlier that the effective, professional policeman is a *flexible* person, one skilled in a variety of actions which he can apply depending on what is appropriate in a given crisis. There are crisis situations, of course, in which you will have no choice of action. For example, the very aggressive, abusive and potentially dangerous citizen who successfully resists your best efforts to calm him down, will make your plan of action necessarily one in which you subdue, restrain and probably arrest him.

In most crisis situations, however, you will have a choice regarding which action plan to follow. We provide below some broad guidelines which can help you choose which plan is most likely to succeed in which situations; but this decision will also have to grow from your own crisis experience on patrol. What works best in each crisis situation will vary to some extent from officer to officer, from citizen to citizen, and from crisis to crisis. Deciding on the best approach for any given officer-citizen-crisis set is a continuing challenge to the professional police officer.

There are five courses of action an officer might follow in a crisis situation: mediate, negotiate, counsel, refer and arbitrate. We wish to now consider each one of these alternatives.

Mediation

Teachers, psychologists, psychiatrists and other professionals who are concerned with helping people solve problems all seem to agree that the most lasting and effective solutions are those that the people themselves come up with. The officer's goal in mediation is to help the citizen solve his own crisis problem, not solve it for him. Rather than giving possible answers or solutions, the mediating officer helps the citizen express what he thinks will work.

In dealing with a husband-wife dispute (where two officers were involved) each officer would, first separately, and then with husband and wife together, encourage and help them. Their goal would be to first have the couple suggest solutions, and then give and take to each other so that they come to an agreement of their own making regarding how the crisis can best be dealt with. The agreement may be not to spend certain monies for liquor again, for the husband to spend the night at a friend's house, to call a given agency in the morning, or something else. The important feature of the solution, however, is that the citizens arrived at the answer themselves, with the officers serving in the role of go-between or mediator.

A report describing a Florida Crisis Intervention Seminar[4] suggests a number of useful guidelines for conducting mediation:

1. If possible, use mediation as your first approach to crisis intervention.
2. Inform the citizens that you cannot solve their problems, that they must do so themselves.
3. Avoid suggesting solutions.

---

[4] Office of the Sheriff. Crisis Intervention Seminar. Jacksonville, Florida, 1975.

4. Elicit suggestions from the citizens as to how their problem can be solved.
5. Check each proposal with the other disputant, until there is acceptance or compromise.
6. Avoid criticizing the citizen's solutions even if you don't agree with them.
7. Offer encouragement for them to follow through.

Negotiation

You will recall that when we described Calming Procedures and, later, Interviewing Procedures, we began with the least directive approaches and went on to describe increasingly forceful, directive police interventions. We wish to follow a similar sequence here, as we describe alternative action plans. In "mediation," the officer is least directive, serving as an encourager and go-between. When this method is either tried and fails, or not tried in the first place because the citizens were in one way or another not ready or able to suggest their own crisis solutions, you must become somewhat more directive. In "negotiation," you do suggest solutions, compromises or other ways of dealing effectively with the crisis. As in mediation, you also help the disputants bargain, and remain neutral as they aid in this give and take.

In a husband-wife dispute, for example, you might suggest a solution to the husband, your partner might do so (separately) with the wife. When the two disputants and you and your partner then come together to reach a joint solution, you can see to it that husband and wife negotiate (with your continued help) according to rules shown elsewhere[5] to be effective steps in successful negotiation:

1. State your position.
2. State your understanding of the other person's position.
3. Ask if the other person agrees with your statement of his position.
4. Listen openly (not defensively) to his response.
5. Propose a compromise.

---

[5] Goldstein, A.P., Sprafkin, R.P., & Gershaw, N.J. *Skill training for community living.* New York: Pergamon Press, 1976.

Counseling

As we mentioned above, when serving as a negotiator, the officer does suggest crisis solutions to the citizens involved. When providing counseling, the officer becomes even more directive. He may not only offer suggestions and advice, but he may help the citizens express and understand both their own and other disputants feelings, wishes, expectations and other less obvious aspects of the crisis. The skilled counselor pays attention, listens carefully, shows interest, observes non-verbal behavior, helps citizens express themselves and, in general, makes use of many of the procedures described earlier in connection with Calming and Interviewing Procedures. The most useful of these procedures for counseling purposes are Showing Understanding, Re-statement of Content, and Reflection of Feeling.

Counseling citizens in crisis takes time. Often it will pay to invest this extra time on a crisis call — both because it helps resolve the crisis and decreases the likelihood of callbacks. But the problems of people in crisis are often very long-standing ones. The marital fight, the de-pressed suicidal person, the drunken citizen all often have long his-tories of their given problem, and thus the problem can't be resolved in a one-shot counseling meeting held under crisis stresses. Thus, the officer-as-counselor will often be doing his job as counselor very well not by resolving the crisis situation, but by opening a door to it, by helping the citizens acknowledge to themselves that a problem exists, and by getting them to agree to do something constructive about it. This "something" will often involve the citizen making use of certain agencies or professional persons in your community. Since the citizen very often does not know about these helping sources, you may do him a great service by skillfully making an appropriate referral — which is the next action plan we wish to describe.

Referral

The officer's first task in skillfully referring someone for further crisis intervention and problem solution is the counseling activity de-scribed above. That is, before you can expect someone to follow re-ferral advice, you must help the person realize that there is a problem which can be helped, and motivate that person to want that help. Your referral will not be a skillful one if your only basis for it is your list of community agencies. You will not be able to adequately describe the full range of services offered by each agency, answer citizen questions about each, or even have a complete enough idea about which agency to recommend at which times, unless you become quite familiar with each one. You are urged to visit these centers and learn more about their nature and functioning. Gradually, you ought to learn about other sources of help in your community for citizens in crisis. Many such sources exist. You ought to become familiar especially with those agencies and people who are the main help-giving sources in the area or areas you usually patrol.

The following guidelines will assist you in making a successful referral:

1. Let the citizen know that you understand his crisis problem and his feelings about it.
2. Tell the citizen that the chances are good that the agency to which you would like to refer him can be of help regarding the crisis problem.
3. Give the citizen, in writing, the appropriate referral information, and make sure he understands it. Use an "Emergency Telephone Numbers" referral card.
4. Deal with any citizen resistance to the referral, e.g., most agencies take people at all salary levels.
5. If possible, have the citizen call the agency when you are still present.
6. If the citizen is too upset or otherwise unable to call the appropriate agency, get his permission for you to make the call, and do so.
7. If circumstances make it inappropriate for either you or the citizen to telephone the agency at the time of your crisis call, obtain a commitment from the citizen (or other person at the crisis scene) that the agency will be contacted at the earliest possible time.

Arbitration

You have tried to help the citizens in crisis solve their own problems (mediation); you have suggested solutions and tried to help them reach a compromise (negotiation); you have tried to help them understand both the problem and what underlies the problem better (counseling); or you have steered them to the appropriate source other than yourself for such help (referral). When all of these alternatives either fail, or are simply inappropriate because one or more of the citizens involved remains highly emotional or aggressive, you may have to directively impose a solution. Such arbitration is clearly not the best means for lasting results. Of the methods examined here it results in the highest number of return calls, probably is the most dangerous of the five action approaches, and, thus, should be used only when clearly necessary.

In arbitration, we recommend the following steps:

1. Consider the strengths and weaknesses of possible solutions to the problem.
2. Try to be aware of your own biases and prejudices, and take account of their effect in your consideration of solutions.
3. Choose the solution you feel is best and, if possible, discuss this choice with your partner.
4. Make a final decision and tell the citizen to do it.

In summary of this section, when **Taking Appropriate Action** you should:

1. **Carefully explain your plan of action to the citizen.**
2. **Check that the citizen understands and agrees with your plan of action.**
3. **Carry out your plan of action.**

CONCLUSION

In this chapter we have described a series of steps we recommend you try to follow when responding to crisis calls. Success in performing these steps will result in a decrease in threats to your safety, reduced citizen emotionalism, more accurate information gathering and, finally, more professional resolution of the crisis. For reference and review purposes, the steps are:

I. **Observing and Protecting against Threats to Your Safety**
   1. **Consider your prior experience on similar calls.**
   2. **Anticipate that the unexpected may actually happen.**
   3. **Form a tentative plan of action.**

II. Calming the Situation
1. Observe and neutralize threats to your safety.
2. Create a first impression of non-hostile authority.
3. Calm the emotional citizen.

III. Gathering Relevant Information
1. Explain to the citizen what you want him to discuss with you and why.
2. Interview the citizen so as to get details of the crisis as clearly as possible.
3. Show that you understand the citizen's statements and give accurate answers to his questions.
4. Revise your plan of action if appropriate.

IV. Taking Appropriate Action
1. Carefully explain your plan of action to the citizen.
2. Check that the citizen understands and agrees with your plan of action.
3. Carry out your plan of action.

II

The Nature of Crisis

Family Disputes

Mental Disturbance

Drug and Alcohol Intoxication

Rape

Suicide

3/ *Family Disputes*

William R. McPeak

Calls for help with family disturbances are common for the police officer, yet often represent one of the tasks he likes least. He may see them as "social work" rather than the crime-fighting type of service he has always thought his job to be. The scenes he enters are confused, and frequently hostile, calling for skills he may have naturally to some degree; but requiring abilities his police training has not given him. He is also limited in the range of interventions he can make by the laws affecting family relations (e.g., he cannot remove a man from his home unless an arrest can be made, or a wife has a court order of protection).

On a more emotional level, the officer's sense of security is shaken when he hears (in police academy or in locker room discussions) about the personal dangers involved in these kinds of calls. Bard (1969) has noted that 22% of police deaths and 40% of police injuries occur while handling family disturbances. The officer also learns quickly that his badge and uniform often can provoke more than reassure, especially when dealing with younger people.

When he does deal with a volatile family problem, he encounters special frustrations. The time and effort he spends settling an issue or cooling a situation seem wasted when he is called back a few hours later, or the next evening. If he does make an arrest as part of his intervention, he may find the complainant turning angrily on him, or withdrawing all charges the next day. In many situations, the complainant may have called the police mainly to scare the offender, using police intervention to exert influence or power. An arrest may mean possible loss of job for the offender and subsequent loss of support for the family, or serious emotional disruption of the family (including the possibility of even more violence when the offender returns home). Unless the complainant experiences a serious and continuing threat, the likelihood is that he or she will be more afraid of arrest and possible detention than repeated injury, once the immediate crisis is past.

If the police officer makes a referral to some community service, he often finds that agency procedures and/or lack of motivation by the family members undo his best efforts. The officer who does find such work to be legitimate and good police service, or who does become skilled at it, may experience a departmental system which seldom recognizes or rewards this part of his work. Yet his reality is that the calls keep coming.

Perhaps the major reason for this is that the police officer is readily available on a 24-hour basis for a family in crisis. He may be the only service poor and undereducated families know. For other families, he represents an intervention with a high likelihood of working. Somehow "the cop" can settle it, by arrest or other force. And, there's no charge. It's free. For a fatherless family, the policeman may be called in periodically as a father-substitute. In the face of violence, he is one of few public servants who both knows how to handle aggressive and dangerous behavior, and who is allowed, by society, to use counter-force (Driscoll, Meyer, and Schanie, 1973).

Even with the increasing availability of social service and mental health crisis teams, the police officer will continue to be a major primary resource for families in stress. This chapter, therefore, intends to provide you with some general ideas about families and their functioning, and about the ways in which they show distress and deal with it.

FAMILY THEORY

Basically, a family is a collection of individuals related by blood and/or legal ties. We assume that these individuals have both special positive meanings (e.g., affection, emotional and financial support) for each other, and some negative, frustrating meanings (e.g., unmet needs, unfulfilled expectations). A family also has a history, which gives members a sense of togetherness and specialness, and often, a long-standing set of difficulties and an inheritance of unresolved problems.

In "normal" families, we assume that there should be general agreement on values (i.e., what is important or preferable to believe or do) and goals (i.e., what we are trying to accomplish as a unit over our years together). There should also be a basic trust and respect for each other, and efforts being made to develop and maintain a positive self-image for each family member. Distinctions between generations should be maintained, in which parents behave as parents, and children or grandparents are not asked to fill that function. And, likewise, society also expects parents to behave as parents, and not as children.

When family members communicate, we expect their messages to be relatively clear, specific, direct and consistent (i.e., various messages "fit" and do not conflict with each other). We expect a minimum of blaming and fruitless "sidetracking" from the real subject of dispute. And we expect some genuine attempts to understand what the other person is saying. The role behaviors we expect of each member should complement the behaviors of other members, provide satisfaction to each person, but remain flexible enough to change as new situations arise in the family.

Another important characteristic of a family is how it functions as a "system." Like an automobile engine which can be studied both for its separate parts, and for its functioning as a collection of those parts, a family can be viewed as it functions as a unit, and, as each individual plays a part, in how, and how well, the unit operates. When dealing with families and other human systems, we also have to face a more complex series of causes of problems. No longer can we simply say that one person said or did something which upset a second person. We know that there may have been certain attitudes or behaviors from the second person which previously influenced the behavior of the first person. Or, there may be problems from other parts of the first person's life (e.g., work difficulties) that are having an important impact on his or her current functioning.

The practical implication of this for you, the officer, and others who have to intervene in family problems is that finding "the bad guy" is a complex task. For example, a husband's drinking and assaultive behavior toward his wife on a given evening may be a response to the emotional frustrations of his work, and sexual frustrations from his wife, who is withholding sex because he drinks and because she is unhappy with his income. He may also be afraid of losing her to another man, with whom she is involved because she views her husband as not meeting her emotional and physical needs.

This type of circular causation (i.e., the response by one person leads to a further response, which leads to yet other responses) is assumed to be part of the functioning of any human system. The work of discovering how and why it is operating in a particular family, especially one in a state of crisis, is time-consuming and generally requires some special methods and insights, few of which are usually available to the officer on patrol. What he is faced with is a volatile situation, involving subtle and complex causes, which he is, nevertheless, required to deal with almost immediately.

A final important idea about a family system is its need for balance, or "homeostasis." This means that the family seeks a minimal degree of upset, and a maximum degree of peacefulness and stability, and will exert a variety of pressures (e.g., guilt-production, anger) to maintain a balance.

FAMILY CRISIS THEORY

Characteristics

There are several important perspectives that may help make a family crisis situation seem less hopeless to the police officer. One set comes from family crisis theory. A crisis is basically defined as "a significant upset in the generally steady, smooth functioning of an individual or a family." By its very nature, a crisis is time limited (i.e., it will tend to resolve itself for better or for worse in a relatively brief period of time, sometimes a few hours, but generally in less than six weeks). The disputants in a family may well come through a general discharge of anger or other feelings, and arrive at some working agreement regarding their problem during the time that the police officer is present.

Another characteristic is that a crisis has some stages you can recognize. These proceed from the initial impact with its highly charged emotions, through a recoil state of denying what's happening, to a resolution stage where some type of solution or accommodation is found.

There are two other characteristics of crisis that are relevant here. The first concerns the way in which an individual interprets an event. An extramarital affair, physical abuse, or an extensive drinking bout may be viewed by one or more parties as relatively "normal," expected and accepted, and therefore hardly worth the degree of upset that seems to be present at that time. Or it may be seen as "vicious," "catastrophic," etc. The *meaning* that the parties in a dispute give to a particular event is therefore an important part of the information you gather during a time of crisis. Once you have this information, you can then move to aid the people involved by suggesting that they might want to consider other possible interpretations of the event.

The other crisis characteristic is that the meaning the individual currently gives to a crisis event is heavily colored by the individual's past experience with similar events. A person raised in a family with an alcoholic parent is likely to view the excessive drinking of a spouse in a different light, and have different fears about what the drinking implies.

When in crisis, family members generally accept help more readily. The amount of distress they feel makes outside help easier to accept, and makes them more ready to find solutions to their problems, whether such solutions are temporary or relatively permanent. Given the idea of homeostasis (a characteristic we discussed earlier), we know that families also seek to restore their former balance, and are generally most willing to re-establish old patterns of relating.

Stress Events

In writing about crisis events in families, Hill (1958) developed three major types of stress events. The first are "accession" events, where a family has to take on a new member, as in the case of an unwanted pregnancy, the return of a parent or child who had left the family, or an addition to a family of a stepmother or stepfather. The second type of crisis is "dismemberment," where a family member is lost, as in desertion, death, separation or divorce. A third type is "demoralization," or events which lead to a loss of family morale, and some degree of family unity. This type would include events that bring disgrace, such as infidelity, non-support, delinquency, alcoholism, or drug addiction.

Hill also discusses a fourth type of event, one which involves demoralization plus accession or dismemberment. This includes runaways, desertion, illegitimacy, divorce, and institutionalization for mental illness. In any of these events, important family changes take place. People must learn to manage feelings of anger, grief, sadness and/or relief. Changes in an individual's self-esteem must be acknowledged, and new role patterns must evolve. As some events are only temporary, it's necessary to maintain some flexibility so that changes can be made again when the particular event is over.

Hill also noted family qualities which he thought were likely to produce good adjustment to crisis. He included flexibility, positive affectional ties, good marital adjustment, generally positive and companionable parent-child relationships, a more democratic style of decision-making, and previous success in dealing with crisis. From reviewing studies focused on family crisis, he found these generalizations:

1. Crisis-proneness is found more among families of low family adequacy (e.g., lack of agreement on family goals, unmet physical and emotional needs).
2. The course of adjustment to crisis is a pattern of disorganization ──→ recovery ──→ readjustment.
3. Family reactions to crisis divide between short-time immediate reactions and secondary long-time adjustments.
4. The more inadequate a family in its organization, the longer will be the time required to adjust after a crisis.
5. Foreknowledge and preparation for a critical event lessens the hardships and improves the chances for recovery (e.g., preparing the children for their parents' separation or divorce).
6. The effects of crisis on a family may be positive or negative, depending on health, wealth, and adequacy possessed by the family (i.e., a family can grow from a crisis also).

FAMILY PATHOLOGY

During the past twenty years, as mental health professionals have attempted to help distressed families, various concepts and descriptions of undesirable family functioning have been developed. Their general purpose has been to describe negative processes between and among family members, processes which are viewed as leading to various types of mental and emotional disorders in individuals, and to painful situations in families. The following concepts do not necessarily describe "types" of families, but rather suggest patterns of behaviors that may be found in troubled families.

"Double Bind" Pattern

One of the first and still best known, of these concepts was that of the "double bind" theory of schizophrenia (Bateson, Jackson, Haley, and Weakland, 1956). This pattern of interaction between two or more people involves conflicting messages. The initial message expresses some positive or negative request. It is followed by a second message which disqualifies or contradicts the first. The contradiction can be verbal, or might be sent on a non-verbal level (e.g., a smile accompanying a statement of hatred). The other characteristic of the double bind situation is that the person receiving conflicting messages is unable or unwilling to comment on the "damned if I do, damned if I don't" situation, or unable to leave the scene.

Such an interactional pattern, especially when it occurs between a parent and child, is destructive in the following way. The victim needs the relationship, wants to view it correctly and communicate back in the right way, but is prevented from commenting on the mixed message by fear of loss of the relationship, and/or denial of his own reality. These contradictory messages occur quite commonly in families, especially in crisis situations. And, at the very least, they represent ambivalence in the individuals involved.

Superego lacunae. There are two other descriptions of family processes that involve some elements of the double bind situation. The first of these is called "superego lacunae" (Giffin, Johnson, and Litin, 1954), which means a gap or deficit in an otherwise good normal conscience. Parents are described as seeking to gratify their own antisocial impulses through the acts of their child. In areas such as truancy, sexual promiscuity, violent behavior toward others, or stealing, the parents forbid the behavior on a conscious level, but unconsciously promote it by methods such as subtle rewards, special attention, or obviously fascinated questioning and warnings.

Scapegoating. The other concept is "scapegoating" (Vogel and Bell, 1960). Here a particular child is unconsciously selected to represent and receive the ills of the parents' marital relationship, and to draw off the interpersonal tension of that relationship. This results in an emotional disturbance or other stress response in that child. This disturbance then diverts attention to the child. In so doing, it relieves parental stress and gives the parents a common object of concern. These children also receive rewards such as special attention or being relieved of responsibilities. Often one parent encourages one type of behavior while the other parent encourages other behavior. The parents are able to see themselves as victims of the child's behavior, which removes the guilt they may feel in victimizing the child.

Schismatic Family

Lidz and his associates at Yale (Lidz, Cornelison, Fleck, and Terry, 1957) discussed two types of families they had seen. They called the first type "schismatic" families. In this situation the marital pair seem to chronically fail to achieve agreement and satisfaction on family goals, affection and roles. The resulting lack of need fulfillment leads to frequent hostile encounters; recurrent threats of separation (which postpone dealing with the problems and cause constant insecurity among family members); and coercive, threatening communications. The parents compete for the children's loyalty and affection to replace missing satisfaction from each other, and to spite each other. And, they frequently criticize one another to the children. A final characteristic is that one or both spouses may show their primary loyalty and affection to their own parents and siblings rather than to their spouse. For example, it is not uncommon for a police officer to find the parents of one marital partner drawn into a dispute, siding with their child against his or her spouse.

Skewed Family

Police may find Lidz's second type of family, designated as "skewed," when called to the crisis scene. Here there is little open conflict, as the home is dominated by the serious psychopathology of one parent, and the family members try very hard to cover up the particular problems that the person has. Police are called when the problems get out of hand temporarily. But, family members generally want the police to handle the matter quickly, and to allow the offender to remain at home.

Triangulation

Another term which describes particular family problems is "triangulation." This term describes a situation where there is a breakdown of an emotional process between two people. In an attempt to stop the breakdown, a third person is brought in, thus forming a triangle. Triangulation may take place either by one or both parties seeking to triangle a third, or by a third person being caught up by the anxiety and entering the emotional process as a stabilizer. It may be evident that the police officer is very often brought in in this way. The positive aspect is that the presence of a third party can help move the pair past their immediate distress with each other to a better interpersonal solution. The negative aspect is that the third party may remain "in" and prevent the original two people from dealing with their emotional stress.

FAMILY VIOLENCE

A common feature of family disturbances is overt aggression which takes place either before or during police intervention. This deliberate use of physical force may be intended solely to inflict pain or injury, and/or to try to get another person to do something which the aggressor wants.

Conflict and tension are a natural part of any human grouping. As we already noted, differing personalities, the stress of unmet needs and unfilled expectations of how others should behave, differing ideas about how the family group should operate and toward what ends, all lead to strain. The family as a group is especially vulnerable in this regard as it has high expectations for intimacy and interpersonal peace, with members bound together both by choice and by love, and by constraints of law and duty. Given the family's importance to its members, the natural human strain and conflict are avoided whenever possible to preserve peacefulness. Yet conflict is not eliminated, but rather temporarily covered over until it often reaches an uncontrollable state, and bursts forth with special fury.

The manifestations of the various stages of violence range from the angry words and family bickering to husbands' and wives' physical attack on one another, excessive bodily punishment of children, and, occasionally, vicious assault and even murder.

While some writers have encouraged "letting it out," or "leveling," to clear the emotional atmosphere in families, Straus's (1974) recent research suggests that expressing verbal aggression directly leads to more aggression rather than to relieving aggression. He suggests that it is better to get the problem "out in the open"; in other words, face the problem, discuss it, and try to reach some workable solution. He believes that "intellectualizing" marital conflicts, and engaging in more rational discussion, produce less physical violence, especially among working class couples.

Police experience with violence tends to be with poor and less-educated families, although these are not the only people who engage in physical aggression. As we noted earlier, such families are more likely to call in social control agents such as police because of awareness, cost, and accessibility. However, there is some evidence that there is a higher incidence of violence in these families. They tend to rely more on physical punishment of their children, which, in the long run, creates a family pattern of aggression. This occurs because of the discipline models the parents present, and because of the impotent hurt and rage the children build up, only to release when they reach adolescence and adulthood. Also, these families often place greater emphasis on the need for physical toughness in children, especially males (see C. Brown, *Manchild in a Promised Land*); and there are generally fewer methods of resolving conflict available in these families.

Steinmetz and Straus (1974) have also discussed violence as a "resource" in families, whereby members who lack other influencing factors such as money, love or respect, may use aggression as a way to maintain their position in a family, and/or as a way to effect changes they seek. These same authors have noted how concerns such as low job satisfaction, large numbers of children, and residential crowding, can create frustration and subsequent violence.

Other authors (e.g., Merton, 1957) have discussed concepts such as "anomie," describing the individual who adopts the values of money or other culturally defined marks of "success" without adopting or adhering to the moral standards or norms of a society. This occurs especially in a society such as ours which holds out the "ends" of successful achievement (i.e., these are the goals that people should reach), but does not offer to certain groups the "means" to achieve these ends. For families in some cultural and ethnic groups, a chronic state of futility, lack of a sense of control of one's own life, and social disconnectedness result.

Goode (1971) has discussed how family members make "exchanges" of loyalty, affection, physical care, obedience, etc., which, hopefully, are experienced as equal and fair by the various family members giving and receiving them. However, one or more persons may begin to feel they are giving more than they are receiving, and engage in conflict with others over this imbalance. Given a human trait of unwillingness to back down or appear weak, disputing individuals will often choose to stand and fight. They reject escape from the situation as a general solution because the need for these relationships is usually great, the costs of leaving are high, and there are strong family and societal pressures to maintain intact families. These same reasons for remaining, of course, bring special hurt and frustration, increasing the likelihood of violence.

Whitehurst (1975) has discussed the strong need for males to exert control over their wives, based on traditional male superiority models and the supposed defeat to male self-esteem from being unable to dominate a relationship. He suggests that the rising emphasis on female equality in areas such as sexual expression, access to extramarital relationships, family decision-making, and career needs, will increase marital frustration, at least in the immediate future, as males and females struggle with the changes.

Some of these same cultural forces also influence parent-child relationships. There is increased frustration in child management as families experience this pressure for full equality. Also, children's friends model varying types of defiance of parents, and may encourage anti-social activities which bring a child, and therefore his family, to a point of conflict with the legal system. Again, the implication of this type of frustration is the experience of anger, inability to control others, and resulting aggression among family members.

Violence Assessment

Mental health professionals have developed a variety of guidelines to assist them in assessing the likelihood of violence, either to one's self (suicide), or to another (homocide). These relate to issues of assessing the intent and probability of aggression occurring; therefore, they are relevant to the police officer (see also Chapter 7).

The first indicator, already discussed in Chapter 2, is the presence of weapons, their accessibility, and their potential to seriously injure or kill. Shoes, bottles, and assorted home furnishings are usually available, but seldom lethal, while the presence or easy accessibility of knives or guns obviously represents a much greater threat.

A second concern is the intent to use such weapons. A highly impulsive, assaultive, or excited person (obvious from his immediate behavior, or his history), is a greater risk than a person who is upset, but still seems in control, and/or has not acted out in the past. (Obviously, a police officer's knowledge of the past patterns of the individuals involved is a major asset in predicting what actions may occur.)

Another factor is the extent of calming resources, either present in the situation or readily available in addition to the police. If a relative or friend who seems minimally antagonistic and generally supportive, is or can be present, this person should be helpful both in settling the participants, and in keeping some degree of calm after the police leave. Also, an immediate or relatively recent crisis is likely to give rise to more intense feelings, and therefore represents a temporarily higher risk of violence. Other high risk situations may include individuals who are manifesting psychotic behavior (see Chapter 4) or drinking heavily (see Chapter 5).

A final note about predicting may prove helpful. The less belligerent person in the dispute, who frequently is the victim at that moment, often has a very good sense of what might happen. You can usually assume that disputes like these have occurred before, though perhaps with somewhat less intensity, and the parties to the dispute have a good idea of the general pattern followed. They often can predict the probable behaviors, their intensity and duration, on the basis of having lived together and learned about each other. They also may have valuable suggestions about what will calm the situation, either through some direct move such as an apology, or through some indirect method such as leaving the home for a cooling-off period, or withdrawing to another room.

POLICE TEAMS

Many family disturbances are covered either by a pair of officers riding together, or by two officers called to the scene to cover each other. Some officers have noted how they have developed certain informal role patterns with a partner, especially someone with whom they have been working for some time. One officer may take a heavy, authoritative role, while the other takes a quiet and more supportive role. In many situations, an officer will take one participant in the dispute to one room while his partner removes the other participant, allowing a cooling-off period for each, and a chance to be listened to and understood.

This type of paired functioning is referred to in family therapy as a "co-therapy team," and some of its characteristics and work are relevant to police teams. For less experienced officers, there is an opportunity to observe a more experienced officer handling family disturbances. Also, one officer can insert himself more directly and strongly into dealing with the problem, while the other is able to stand back and watch the total situation, both for safety reasons, and to observe and note events or issues his partner doesn't notice. In this situation, the family may be more free to struggle with one officer to get a problem resolved, while relying on the other to steady the scene, if necessary. After leaving a family disturbance, there is also the opportunity to discuss what occurred, and develop new and better ways to handle similar situations in the future.

To make this type of team functioning most constructive, the partners need to have a general liking and respect for each other. And, they need to develop an ability to be open with each other, both for support and for constructive criticism. The partners need to be able to ask each other for help and to allow one to be dominant for a while without the other feeling subservient. The officers should discuss the types of family disputes they feel especially competent and comfortable with, as well as those that they feel uncomfortable with. In this way they can bring the best possible resources to the problem. In other words, an officer can take a more passive role in a situation where he feels unusually threatened, or a more active role where he feels more sure of himself. It's important to remember, though, that the very nature of many of these calls leaves little time to discuss and carefully assign each officer.

USE OF COMMUNITY SERVICES

Parnas (1967) has noted that "both the common family argument and the more serious one that involves the police grow out of the mundane problems of family-living: finances, alcohol, infidelity, family discipline, or more trivial matters. It is the exaggerated response by one or more parties to these common disputes that results in police interference in what was formerly a family matter" (p. 915). As is true of many of the problems individuals and families struggle with, the "trivial matters" and "common disputes" are only symptoms of a more pervasive and deeper problem in a marriage or family. Fighting over drinking, late hours, or undesirable companions is usually part of more significant issues involving the participants' self-esteem, trust, ability to influence or control others and personal security.

Resolving the immediate presenting problem is highly desirable, and often a very real service. But, police and family members need to recognize that at some time they may need to address and resolve more basic issues if possible. One resource for this is the informed use of community agencies offering individual, marital and family counseling, and specialized legal and social services. While some authors have called for guidance for the police as to *types* of families most likely to accept such referrals, a more successful step may be to make sure that police officers are completely informed about the services and eligibility requirements of different agencies. This initial good matching of problem, participants, and service agency is more likely to make a good and lasting referral. But referrals can fail. The family in crisis, at first receptive to referral, often loses motivation after a volatile evening or the passage of a few days.

The majority of family disturbances are non-criminal in nature; and therefore, referral after calming by the police is frequently the next most appropriate step. This suggests that (given the high incidence of family disturbance calls police departments receive), a substantial amount of time in initial training and on-going education should be devoted to giving knowledge of the variety of service agencies and the ways in which they are best used.

Another valuable resource may be to have police officers who are specialized resource agency people, available round-the-clock. There are also mental health or other crisis services which can advise police or even interview the family. These types of services are now available in many large cities, and are well used by police, especially once police officers and agency personnel come to a good understanding of each other's skills and job responsibilities. Interacting in this way can also help to identify needed services and can provide some cross-training of each professional group.

SUMMARY

Insights from family theory (e.g., the family's need for stability, the complex interacting causes in a crisis situation) and family pathology (e.g., "double bind" messages being given, "scapegoating" of one family member by others) should help you see the variety of factors present in a family disturbance which you are facing. And information from studies on violence in families should help to explain some of the uncomfortable and threatening aggressive behaviors that may be occurring.

The perspectives from family crisis theory (e.g., the impact of individual meanings given to "upsetting" behaviors, the time-limited nature of crisis) and from violence assessment (e.g., degree of impulsiveness, presence of other calming persons) can guide you in how you will proceed in a stressful situation. After judging the potential situation, you (and a partner, if available) should now be able to get clear, specific and minimally aggressive communication working. You can explore the nature and meanings of a particular incident, and get a sense of the pattern that usually evolves in this kind of situation. Then, you can engage the participants in productive problem-solving at that moment. If other community resources such as social service agencies seem indicated, you can assist the family to find those that will be most appropriate.

References

Bard, M. Family intervention: Police teams as a community mental health resource. *Journal of Criminal Law, Criminology, and Police Science*, 1969, 60, 247-250.

Bateson, G., Jackson, D., Haley, J., & Weakland, J. Toward a theory of schizophrenia. *Behavioral Science*, 1956, 1, 241-264.

Brown, C. *Manchild in a promised land*. New York: Macmillan, 1965.

Driscoll, J., Meyer, R., & Schanie, C. Training police in family crisis intervention. *Journal of Applied Behavioral Science*, 1973, 9, 62-82.

Giffin, M., Johnson, A., & Litin, E. Specific factors determining antisocial acting-out. *American Journal of Orthopsychiatry*, 1954, 24, 668-684.

Goode, W. Force and violence in the family. *Journal of Marriage and the Family*, 1971, 33, 624-636.

Hill, R. Social stresses on the family: Generic features of families under stress. *Social Casework*, 1958, 39, 139-150.

Lidz, T., Cornelison, A., Fleck, S., & Terry, D. The intrafamilial environment of schizophrenics: Marital schism and marital skew. *American Journal of Psychiatry*, 1957, 114, 241-248.

Merton, R. Continuities in the theory of social structure and anomie. In *Social theory and social structure*. New York: Free Press of Glencoe, 1957.

Parnas, R. The police response to the domestic disturbance. *Wisconsin Law Review*, 1967, 914-960.

Steinmetz, S., & Straus, M. General introduction: Social myth and social system in the study of intrafamily violence. In S. Steinmetz & M. Straus (Eds.), *Violence in the family*. New York: Dodd, Mead & Company, 1975.

Straus, M. Leveling, civility, and violence in the family. *Journal of Marriage and the Family*, 1974, 36, 13-29.

Vogel, E., & Bell, N. Emotionally disturbed child as the family scapegoat. In N. Bell & E. Vogel (Eds.), *A modern introduction to the family*. Glencoe, Ill: The Free Press, 1960.

Whitehurst, R. Violence in husband-wife interaction. In S. Steinmetz & M. Straus (Eds.), *Violence in the family*. New York: Dodd, Mead & Company, 1975.

4/ *Mental Disturbance*

Joseph T. Himmelsbach

Since man began observing, recording and describing how other men behave, there has been evidence of what modern man has labeled "mental illness." Every period has had its method of categorizing those individuals who acted in a different way than the majority. Some were called mystics, some were called heretics, some were called witches, some were called lunatics, but now they are called the mentally ill. Although past cultures explained strange behavior in different ways (e.g., being in league with Satan); and, although the "cures" used were also varied and often harsh (e.g., being burned at the stake), some of the behaviors which the afflicted person exhibited were remarkably similar to those which we now call mental illness.

These behaviors include feelings of omnipotence or persecution; strange ideas, feelings or sensations; poor relationships with others; and various kinds of bizarre behavior. Thus, mental illness has been a complex, ever present aspect of our society. No existing simple solutions have been effective in reducing its occurrence. It is an extensive problem insofar as it touches, to some degree, one out of every twenty persons in the United States at some point in their lives.

Prior to the advent of modern treatment techniques in the 1960's, half of the hospital beds in the United States were occupied by mentally ill individuals. The picture is not much brighter today, even though fewer of the mentally ill wind up in hospitals. Since the police are frequently called to respond to the mentally ill person, it is necessary that they have some understanding of mental illness, as well as of effective techniques for dealing with it.

As with many other community situations involving police, this is a problem for which police have extensive responsibility, but little training. For example, fully 50% of admissions to mental health facilities in the Baltimore area in a given year were the result of a police referral (Liberman, 1969). Other communities have reported similar statistics. This is due partly to the fact that in most communities mental health resources are not readily accessible during evening and weekend hours. In another, more comprehensive survey, Hollingshead and Redlich (1958) found that in the lower socio-economic classes, more than half of the persons receiving mental health services were referred by the police. In addition, 90% of those people who called police for assistance with a mentally ill person indicated that, if necessary, they would do so again.

As in other "social problem" situations, many police officers do not view dealing with mentally ill persons as one of their obligations. A majority of communities do not agree with this view. Police are expected to assist with the mentally ill because of the latter's potential for violence and their frequent disturbance of public order. Besides, police ordinarily come into contact with individuals who exhibit a high level of deviancy from the norm of accepted behavior. In each of these contacts, the officer will be expected to make judgments, engage in some activity, and satisfactorily resolve the problem so that the disturbance will be minimized.

This can be a most difficult and complex task, made more difficult by the fact that it must be completed rather quickly, and usually without either benefit of information about the person's past history or a professional consultation. Therefore, it becomes absolutely necessary that police officers understand the causes and symptoms of mental illness, as well as techniques which make their contacts with mentally ill persons more effective.

CAUSES OF MENTAL ILLNESS

There is not one identifiable cause for mental illness. It is even difficult to develop a generally acceptable definition of the term itself. To some people, such as Thomas Szasz, "mental illness" does not exist, but rather, is a way for certain individuals to "control" people whom they feel are different or strange, or who behave in ways not in keeping with society's norms. Dr. Szasz feels that mental illness is a useless, meaningless concept that should not be applied to anyone.

At the other extreme, there is the view held by certain psychiatrists that almost everyone has some level of mental disorder which impedes their daily functioning. Such disorders range from phobias and neuroses to full-blown psychotic episodes. These theorists view mental illness as a "real" disease, just like heart disease or diabetes, which they feel can be treated effectively with medical intervention.

A majority of mental health practitioners hold that some form of "personal disturbance" does exist in many persons, and that it can be treated. However, they may not agree that the problem is entirely a medical one. Due to this conflict in theory and practice, it appears at times to an outside observer or layman that mental health workers are almost as confused as the patients they serve.

More confusion is added to attempts to define mental illness when you consider the cultural criteria which are used in determining whether or not a person is mentally ill. The standard which is frequently invoked is that the person "is not acting properly or appropriately." Usually this means that given a person's position and responsibilities in life, and the way he is acting, he is not meeting people's expectations of the norm.

Sometimes these judgments are based on the person's apparent social class. For example, a person who has been wandering around the streets, intoxicated, sleeping in doorways, is a common sight in our large urban centers. If observers perceive that such a person is a "street bum" and has been for many years, they may feel pity for the individual, but not an overwhelming concern. However, if the person happens to be a well-respected businessman with strong family ties, etc., most observers would judge that the person has "gone off the deep end" and needs immediate psychiatric help.

What is expected of another person may also be determined by one's culture. Each culture and ethnic grouping in the United States has certain rituals and superstitions which they feel are proper and correct. However, once these rituals are transferred to another culture, they may appear bizarre or become suspect. Religious or superstitious practices which are accepted beliefs in some cultural groups, such as the feeling that certain individuals are born with the "evil eye" and can inflict misfortune on others, may be perceived as being delusional in other groups located in different sections of the country.

Finally, *where* certain behavior occurs also can influence whether others consider it acceptable or bizarre. People can go to church on Sunday and "talk to God." However, if they are sitting on a park bench and "talking to God," others around them are very likely to view their behavior as strange. In another case, a group of grown men can dress up in funny costumes, ride around the streets in "kiddie cars," cause general havoc, but not be considered bizarre as long as they belong to the same fraternal organization. If another person were to act in exactly the same way, but not as a member of the group, and not on parade day, he would probably be escorted off to see the psychiatrist.

It is impossible to divorce the concept of mental illness from these social and cultural issues. Although someone who is mentally ill may be experiencing some personal difficulties, these difficulties usually are displayed to the world by the person's inability to conform to society's expectations. Because of the difficulty in defining mental illness in abstract terms, it is necessary to focus on more observable behaviors which may indicate its presence. A suggested behavioral definition of mental illness would be, "any action that is taken by an individual which is inappropriate to his or her present situation, which has no potential for achieving the stated goal of the action, and which continues despite objective, accurate information that such action is unlikely to be effective."

Thus, for example, if a person's stated goal is his desire to become governor of a state, then objectively, his running in and out of state offices, stealing papers and pens will not achieve it. Another example would be a mother stating that she is concerned about her children's health, so she is not allowing them to eat any food in her house, even though other people have eaten the food without harm.

Defining mental illness in this manner does not remove the influence of the socio-cultural variables mentioned earlier, but it does lessen their impact. It also points out the advantages of the observer having exposure to certain kinds of life experiences, in order to be better able to make judgments as to what is appropriate in certain situations. In this regard, the experienced, veteran police officer would have an advantage over the inexperienced, not yet "street wise," rookie. Most police officers with whom this author has had contact have exhibited a working knowledge of human behavior which allows them to make fairly accurate judgments as to the appropriateness of certain behaviors. Many times they are not able to clearly describe the concepts behind such judgments, but this does not lessen their accuracy.

Given this working definition of mental illness, we will explore certain factors which contribute to its occurrence. The three general factors which are most often held to contribute to the development of mental illness are: heredity, learning and history, and environment.

Heredity

There is much debate about the genetic factors which may influence the development of mental illness. To date, research has not established a direct causative link between the presence of mental illness in a parent or parents, and the emergence of mental illness in their children. However, there have been several well-formulated studies which have shown that there can be a tendency to certain forms of mental disturbance if one or both parents have had a history of mental disorder.

Wender (1969) completed a study of the children of schizophrenic parents who were raised either by their own parents or adoptive parents, and found that both sets of children had a higher incidence of schizophrenia than a comparison normal group. The children raised by adoptive parents had the genetic make-up of their natural parents, who were schizophrenic, but were not raised in the "schizophrenic" environment. Their developing symptoms of schizophrenia was attributed to their heredity. This study did not prove a direct cause and effect relationship between schizophrenic parents having schizophrenic children, but rather, indicates a genetic predisposition for those offspring to develop that problem.

Learning and History

The second factor which plays a major role in the development of mental disturbance is the combination of the learning experiences and personal history of the individual. Significant personal events in every individual's life play a powerful role in changing a person's feelings, attitudes and beliefs. When these events have a negative emotional impact, the end result may be that the person will develop some form of disordered behavior. Examples of historical events which can lead to such effects are the deaths of one or both parents during childhood or adolescence, the absence of an intact family unit, the presence of school or discipline problems, the presence of sexual difficulties during puberty, the presence of family alcoholism, as well as traumatic medical problems or illnesses. These are but a few of the many stresses which people may experience during their development which may have a detrimental effect on their later functioning.

Learning refers to the methods and skills which people develop to cope with the world around them. Every person acquires certain skills which he or she utilizes for coping with the stresses and strains of everyday life, as well as for insuring that his or her needs be satisfied. Learning these skills begins at infancy and continues through adolescence and adulthood. Such learning is affected early in life by the inputs which parents provide, and the expectancies for certain behavior which their environment places on them. Many times the maladaptive behaviors people learn during this period become inflexible and unchanging. For example, it is appropriate and sometimes considered "cute," when an 8-year-old gets angry and has a tantrum in response to not getting his own way. However, if parents do not "teach" this child that as he matures he must develop alternate ways of expressing his frustration, and make no effort to teach the child these alternatives, he may become a 28-year-old who throws temper tantrums.

Another example of the same principle is that children learn how to be parents from observing how their parents treated them. It is a fact that parents who are child abusers very often were themselves abused as children. This definitely has no genetic link, but rather is a function of learning how to deal with a child who is causing a disturbance in the home. Thus both "good" and "bad" ways of coping with the world are learned during childhood and adolescence. If what is learned during this period contributes to a person being a more effective adult, that person will be less likely to experience severe emotional problems as an adult.

Environment

The final contributor to mental illness is the individual's present environment. Genetic, historical and learning factors set the foundation for the person to interact with his environment. However, events in the environment often serve as the immediate stressors which cue off the development of emotional problems. Individuals who show signs of emotional disturbance will usually report an unusual or overwhelming stress occurring just prior to the onset of symptoms. Such precipitating stresses could be the loss of a job, a dispute with close family members, or other threats to an individual's sense of security. When people seek out psychiatric help, it is usually for these "stress reasons." It is very rare for an individual to go to a therapist to improve his "poor upbringing" as a child. Rather, the person usually has some difficulty in dealing with his present life situation, which may or may not relate to the fact that he has had negative childhood experiences.

The model described above is very complex. All of the factors mentioned influence whether or not a person develops emotional disturbance. Any individual factor can produce signs of mental disturbance even when the other two seem normal. For example, extreme environmental stress can produce psychiatric symptoms in anyone. This was observed in World War II when soldiers who were quite normal before a battle developed "battle fatigue" after being under siege for three to four days without proper rest or food. Fortunately, once the stress was removed and they were given a chance to rest and eat properly, the symptoms in all but a small minority of cases disappeared in a matter of days.

Likewise, any of the three factors can help neutralize any of the others. The effect of poor interpersonal relationships in childhood and adolescence can be limited by strong, secure interpersonal contacts in adulthood. In summary, one should view the causes of mental disturbance as a complex, interactive process. It probably involves genetic matters, the past history and learning experience of the individual, and the everyday events which that individual encounters.

TERMS OF MENTAL DISTURBANCE

There are many terms which are used to describe people who are mentally ill. Many of these terms have become part of our common language in describing troubled people, terms such as "paranoid" or "psychotic." Unfortunately, these descriptions are often used inaccurately without proper understanding of what they mean. Since the police officer will probably be hearing these terms from the mental health workers with whom he has professional contact, and since some of the individuals he will be dealing with will be described to him in this fashion, he should have an accurate, professional, working knowledge of them. We will explain five of the most common descriptive terms. Then in the next section, we will describe the specific symptoms which indicate that a person is experiencing an emotional problem.

Psychosis and Neurosis

Two of the most frequently used descriptive terms are "psychotic" and "neurotic." Both are broad terms which serve to indicate the relative severity of an individual's problem. A psychotic person is usually much more seriously disturbed than a neurotic individual; and, it is more common for police officers to deal with psychotic persons than neurotic persons. The latter group primarily has contact with police when they contemplate suicide.

Psychotic individuals are those people who are not able to view or respond to the world around them in an objectively realistic fashion. They often display disorders in their ability to think and reason clearly. The thoughts which control their actions are frequently illogical. Their impairment in the ability to deal with the world realistically is often so severe that their welfare and safety, or that of others, is frequently threatened. When a person is psychotic, it does not mean that he is unable to listen to or respond to other people. Many times a psychotic person is able to engage in a regular conversation on topics which are not part of his psychotic system. Also, a psychotic person's language is not necessarily gibberish which only he can understand. The person uses and pronounces words in the same fashion as other people in his environment. However, when he uses the words in a sentence or a statement, they may not quite make sense. Something may appear to be missing. This missing part is usually the logical connecting message in the statement.

A neurotic person, on the other hand, is someone whose reasoning and thinking processes are pretty much intact. Their health and safety are usually not threatened by their difficulty. The problems which they express are primarily internal conflicts between two different, competing drives; for example, the wish to be loved, yet the desire to be independent from, and not responsible to the other person. Neurotic individuals are able to carry out their everyday activities of job, school or housework, but report feeling uncomfortable or anxious or deeply unhappy. There is a kernel of truth in the folk saying, "Neurotics build castles in the air while psychotics live in them."

Schizophrenia

"Schizophrenia" is a formal diagnosis which implies a collection of certain symptoms. It is a severe form of mental disturbance, and a diagnosis given to about half the patients on inpatient psychiatric services. The reason we discuss it here is to correct a common layman's misconception that schizophrenia means "split personality," or "Dr. Jekyll and Mr. Hyde." It does not.

People who feel that the schizophrenic is a person with a "split personality" usually become very frightened when they have to deal with a person who is so afflicted. They fear that the person may suddenly change into his other personality and become quite dangerous. This is not the case. The term schizophrenic means that the person is cut off from his emotional experiences and his rational thought processes, as well as from close interpersonal contacts with people around him. This is what he has "split" from, it is not a "split personality." Such separation from feelings and other people tends to make a person more lonely and frightened, not frightening.

Paranoia

The other term which is frequently used but often misunderstood, is "paranoid." Usually one hears it in the phrase "dangerous paranoid." Unfortunately, the two terms, dangerous and paranoid, have tended to become synonomous due to their frequent use together. A paranoid person is one who views himself as occupying a special, important position in his environment in relation to other people. In its extreme form the individual may take on the role of a very important person, such as a religious savior or a noted political figure.

However, he usually is the only person who believes that he occupies this "celebrity" position.

The people around him usually view him quite differently. As a result, the paranoid person may become suspicious of these other people since, if "they are not with me," then "they must be against me." A paranoid person's view of himself may, thus, include the feelings that he is the world's greatest (delusions of grandeur) and the world's most hated (delusions of persecution) person. It should be noted that paranoid people can become dangerous because they may feel threatened by those around them. They then may view their only hope as being able to "fight" against their enemies. Suffice it to say that some paranoid people can become dangerous, but this is certainly not true of all paranoid individuals.

Catatonia

Finally, a less frequently used, but not uncommon term is "catatonic." It is used to describe individuals who have withdrawn from their environment to such a degree that they become very rigid and stiff in posture and gait. They stop communicating, not speaking or uttering any sound for days, weeks or in some severe cases, even months. The catatonic person usually becomes this way when he feels totally overwhelmed by his own feelings, for example, sexual or aggressive feelings. Many persons who become catatonic are capable of losing control quite suddenly. This is known as a "catatonic excitement," and occurs when the person's rage, which has been bottled up inside, can no longer be contained. It then becomes expressed in an overwhelming rush of behavior, frequently aggressive or destructive.

SYMPTOMS OF MENTAL DISTURBANCE

The schizophrenic, paranoid, neurotic or catatonic person may show one or more common symptoms of mental disorder, symptoms which we wish to describe below.

Anxiety

Anxiety is probably the most common symptom in any form of emotional disturbance. The person reports feeling "jumpy," "on edge," "having butterflies in the stomach," or feeling "tightly wound up." The anxious person usually has trembling hands, sweaty palms and a dry mouth. Anxiety usually accompanies situations that are unusual, strange, fearful or threatening. Everyone has experienced anxiety at frequent points during his or her life, e.g., before getting married, or when asking the boss for a raise. However, it becomes pathological and an indicator of emotional distress when there is no apparent, objective reason for its occurrence.

Depression

Depression is evident in many forms of emotional disturbance. And the person who is depressed is characterized by a number of things. His actions slow down, he eats and sleeps poorly, talks less than normal, appears sad and distressed, and reports feeling "blue" or "down in the dumps." You will find a more comprehensive outline of the symptoms of depression in Chapter 7, which deals with suicide.

Confusion

The person who is confused has a reduced awareness of his surroundings. He is unable to focus on particular topics or interactions. He may appear preoccupied with certain events or thoughts. Because he is confused, his actions may be dangerous to himself or others, e.g., turning on a gas stove, but forgetting to light it. You should be aware that confusion can be caused by things other than mental disturbance. The same symptom can be the result of diabetic coma, stroke, alcohol or drug intoxication, or other cerebral trauma.

Fear

This refers to an unreasonable fear of certain people, such as family members, clergymen or the police. It may also be generalized to certain situations, for example, being alone or entering a room. The fear is usually expressed by the person experiencing a sense of dread or danger that something terrible is about to happen to him.

Obsessions

Obsessions are recurrent thoughts over which the person apparently has no control. These thoughts are bothersome to the individual and may make him quite uncomfortable. Usually the obsessive material relates to actions that the person finds unacceptable. The individual may have thoughts of harming himself or someone else, or he may have thoughts about sexual activities or practices which are threatening to him, e.g., homosexual thoughts. Obsessions are usually accompanied by a high level of anxiety.

Anger

Anger does not refer to the appropriate expression of anger by individuals on an everyday basis, but rather to an extreme hypersensitivity to comments from other people. The person may view almost every comment made by others as an insult or attack. The individual may behave in a very argumentative way, challenging every statement anyone offers.

Mania

Mania is frequently seen in a particular psychotic disorder known as Manic-Depressive Psychosis. The person experiences rapid and extreme mood swings from depression to mania. In the latter situation the person is joyful, grandiose and magnanimous. Persons in a manic state are "everybody's friend." They may frequently spend large amounts of money with little thought, running up large debts. They may report staying awake and active for periods of two to three days. Sexual activity may increase, and the person's judgment as to what is harmful to him becomes impaired.

Social Withdrawal

A person displaying social withdrawal will remove himself from almost all contact with others in his environment. This includes his family and close friends, as well as passing acquaintances and strangers. In its less extreme form, the person becomes somewhat unresponsive to social demands and social amenities, such as greeting people when they enter a room, or engaging in polite conversation.

Hallucinations

When someone hallucinates, he or she experiences an event which has no objective, realistic source. For example, the individual may hear voices or see things which don't actually exist. Hallucinations can be evidence of severe mental disorders, but may also indicate that the person is experiencing problems in brain functioning. Hallucinations can occur in people who ingest drugs or have been drinking for extensive periods (D.T.'s). The experience can occur with all of the senses; but, the most common hallucinatory experiences usually are visual and auditory. Do not confuse hallucinations with illusions. The latter occur when actual, objective events are misinterpreted due to a poor perception of them. For example, a person may report seeing "a ghost" in the shadows of a tree, but on later investigation discover that it was a sheet of white paper stuck in a tree limb.

Delusions

These are personal beliefs about persons, events or situations which are objectively untrue, but which the person holds to be accurate despite substantial, conflicting information. Delusions are attempts by individuals to redefine their world in order that they have more control over it, or to make it less threatening to themselves. An example of a delusion would be a person's belief that a group of people were poisoning his water supply in order to make him impotent. This is an upsetting thought, but in this example may serve to cover the person's intense fear that he may be sexually inadequate.

Impaired Social Performance

This is a general symptom to which we referred earlier. It is evidenced by the person being unable to carry out his expected role and responsibilities. The family breadwinner does not go to work, but rather spends the day sleeping; the student drops out of school to watch T.V. all day; the housewife refuses to care for her family.

Disorientation

Disorientation refers to the person who is unaware of where he is, what time it is, or who he is. This is another sign which can also indicate some form of brain damage, as well as psychological impairment.

Inappropriate Affect

An individual's "affect" refers to the manner in which he displays his feelings and mood. Appropriate affect is when the person's mood fits the situation he is experiencing. For example, people should be sad and cry at funerals, they should be happy and excited if they have won a lottery. Inappropriate affect is present when a person's mood and expression do not fit the situation he is experiencing, e.g., laughing and being happy at a funeral, being indifferent in a threatening situation, etc.

Impaired Reality Contact

This is a summarizing term which is used when a specific group of symptoms is present. The person may be expressing himself in a manner that no one can understand. He may be extremely suspicious of other people's actions or motivations. He may have difficulty telling the difference between external real events and internal subjective events. He may feel that others can read his mind. Or he may show other severe symptoms of mental disturbance.

The symptoms described above cover most of what you should be familiar with in telling the difference between those people who are severely mentally ill and those who are not. When you are familiar enough with such behavior to make an accurate judgment that you are dealing with a mentally ill person, we urge you to implement the suggestions which follow dealing with effective interventions with such persons.

THE DANGER FACTOR

One of the most frequently raised concerns of police officers who deal with the mentally disturbed individual is how potentially dangerous the person is. Police officers, as well as people in general, commonly hold the view that if a person is "mental" then they must be homicidally dangerous. Support for this erroneous view is provided by the occasional newspaper accounts of ex-mental patients shooting five passers-by "for no reason," or the gruesome description of family murders, the perpetrator of which "has a history of psychiatric problems." These individual accounts are frequently sensationalized in the media, and are shared nationally by news services. The unfortunate consequence is that the problem of mental illness becomes minimized, while the problem of dangerousness becomes maximized.

The factual, objective relationship between mental disturbance and degree of dangerousness is that mentally ill persons, as a group, are *less* dangerous to other people than the population in general is. Concretely, this means that you are more likely to be hurt while walking the streets, by a citizen who has not been diagnosed as being mentally ill, and less likely to be hurt by someone who does have a history of mental disturbance. Naturally, every experienced officer will probably be able to cite examples of so-called "raving lunatics" who battled several officers hand-to-hand for thirty minutes before being subdued. These officers should reflect on the number of occasions they have had a similar experience while apprehending a non-psychotic criminal, or breaking up a family fight.

Another myth about the mentally ill person is that when he becomes disturbed he has the "strength of ten men." Again, there is no scientific or objective support for this view. Of course, a person's adrenalin level may be higher due to his fright and anxiety, which would allow him greater endurance or a burst of extra energy. However, this does not transform him into a "superman." Also, the mentally ill person who "acts out" may have no regard for social controls, or may lack self-control for his actions. He may engage in aggressive actions which are disorganized and frantic, thus giving the impression of being a "wild man."

Factual studies indicate that when police are involved with mentally ill persons, the persons are much more often than not, non-violent. Liberman (1969) found that the typical patient with whom the police had contact was either schizophrenic or suffered from a personality disorder, but was not violent. Bitner (1967) points out that "in most cases [the] patients are passively compliant, or at least manageable by means of verbal influence" (p. 284). Steadman (1974) recently completed a study of patients who were released from a facility for the criminally insane. He followed a group of 199 male patients who were supposedly "mentally ill and dangerous," and found that in a four-year period following their release, only 20% of the group were involved in any assaultive behavior.

The conclusion we can draw is that for a majority of your contacts with mentally ill persons, your life or safety will not be jeopardized. Please note that this does not mean that you should not exercise good judgment and take prudent action to insure your safety. It does not mean that mentally ill persons can never be dangerous. But the likelihood of violence is not nearly as great as often believed.

LEGAL ISSUES IN POLICE CONTACTS
WITH THE MENTALLY ILL

Every state has statutes which describe the specific authority and responsibility that police officers have in dealing with mentally ill persons. In most states, statutes exist which allow the officer to take an individual into custody whom the officer feels is mentally ill, and is acting in a harmful or dangerous manner to himself or others. Once the person is in custody, the laws generally allow the officer to transport the individual for purposes of a committal examination. In certain states, the decision to send a person to a psychiatric facility involuntarily, rests with the local county attorney or prosecuting attorney. He may make this decision based on the evidence which the apprehending officer provides him.

In other states, the officer may transport the person to a physician or physicians who will make a medical/legal decision as to the need for hospitalization. If they decide to commit an individual, this committal decision can be reviewed through the courts at the patient's request. This procedure insures that the person's rights and liberties are not infringed upon. Following the person's committal to a psychiatric facility, the officer may be involved in transporting such individuals to committal facilities.

Since it is impossible to review here all of the relevant laws in any meaningful way, each reader should make an effort to become familiar with the appropriate sections of mental hygiene law for his jurisdiction. You should focus particular attention on specific sections which clearly define your responsibilities and authority. Secondly, you should become familiar with the procedures, both voluntary and involuntary, for admitting people to psychiatric facilities in your state.

PROCEDURE FOR MANAGING THE DISTURBED PERSON

As in every police situation, you should begin preparing your response to assist a mentally disturbed person prior to your arrival at the scene. Your first step should be to consider what you wish the outcome of the contact to be. In most situations, your goal would be threefold:

1. to assess whether the person is mentally disturbed, and if he is,
2. to see that he gets to a mental health agency for treatment, while
3. insuring that no harm comes to the patient, bystanders or yourself.

If you keep these three goals in mind, you'll find it easier to work through these frequently chaotic and complex situations.

Safety

When you arrive at a scene, your first concern should be the safety of everyone present — the patient, family members, strangers, fellow officers, you yourself. Concern for safety should begin prior to your arrival on the scene. If you have information that the person in question is mentally disturbed, then you should prepare yourself psychologically for a situation which will probably be confusing and anxiety provoking.

Secondly, we suggest that you attempt to review in your mind the characteristics and behaviors of mentally ill persons outlined earlier. This will help you to be more sensitive to any cues which the person may give about his difficulties or his planned actions. You must present a calm, in-charge attitude. Most likely, the people who have contacted the authorities will feel that the situation is difficult to control, and will probably be somewhat distraught. You will have to calm these people before you will be able to approach the disturbed subject. You may have to move troublesome family members away from the scene.

By dealing with family and bystanders first, you can gain information about the problem and secure the area prior to making contact with the subject. Keep in mind that in responding to mentally ill persons, hasty or ill-conceived action can be more harmful than no action at all. No one ever died from mental illness. Unless some actively dangerous or life-threatening situation exists, you have the time to obtain information before responding to the citizen.

The information which you should try to gather from family and friends is specific. You should ask about the person's present state — is he agitated, calm, assaultive, withdrawn, communicative, armed? Next, find out about his recent and past history. Has he ever been like this before? If yes, how was it handled? Does he have a long standing psychiatric problem? Is he being treated for it and by whom? Has his therapist been contacted? Were there any particular events that precipitated this emotional outburst? Are there any persons who have a calming, trustful relationship with the individual? Are they present?

The goal of this questioning is to provide you with relevant information which will help you formulate some ideas about the citizen, his problems, and how best to deal with him. You can frequently use the therapist or trusted friend as an ally to make contact with the individual. This person can introduce you to the subject, thus making your presence legitimate, and reducing the threat the subject may feel. The above information can usually be gathered in five to ten minutes.

There are occasions when you will respond to a call without informants being present. For example, a person who is disturbed may be secluded in a small apartment, and the police may receive a call from his landlord to have the person evicted for non-payment of rent. In that situation, you will have to operate "blindly" until you begin to make contact with the subject. The techniques to be described next are appropriate for either situation.

Although involvement with a mentally ill person is not usually dangerous, you should position yourself in relation to the individual in such fashion as to minimize the possibility of being struck or hit by flying objects. If the person has barricaded himself in a room and has firearms, you should initiate whatever actions are necessary to secure the area before attempting to "talk the guy down." Again, unless someone's life or safety is at stake, don't attempt to rush the subject and overpower him.

It is helpful to keep in mind that most mentally ill persons are frightened or extremely fearful. You should approach such an individual as if you were approaching a frightened animal you were trying to rescue. You would not attempt to rush in and grab the animal while yelling and screaming at it. Instead, you would make slow cautious moves, talking to the animal in a quiet, calming voice, all the while easily approaching it. The same principles hold when you're dealing with a frightened human being who is mentally disturbed.

Assuming that you have established a safe environment, collected as much information as possible, and begun developing the atmosphere described above, you are now well-prepared to begin working with the subject. Remember your goals: be non-threatening, and safely move the individual out of danger to a professional treatment setting. You can achieve these goals by establishing honest, truthful and understanding communication between yourself and the individual. Your opening statement should be in two parts: first, introduce yourself by name; and second, state why you are there.

This latter statement could take one of the following forms: "I've been asked to talk to you by your family because they're concerned about you. What seems to be going on?" Or, "Your friends have said that you've been having some difficulties, what's your side of the story?" You should try to avoid opening with questions which have simple yes or no answers, such as, "Do you want to talk now?" After you introduce yourself and ask the first few questions, if the individual begins to talk, you should allow him some period of time to vent any of the pent-up feelings or emotions he may have. In a sense, you should allow the person to "get it off his chest."

On many occasions you will not have to ask any opening questions, since the person will begin immediately to present his view of the problem. During these opening interchanges, you should be sensitive to any indicators that he is feeling threatened, either by you or by others. If you begin to sense this, make it very clear that you are not going to harm him or hurt him in any way. In addition, if he feels threatened by others, you have the benefit of being seen as the public protector by a majority of citizens. You can build on this role and state the following: "I am a police officer and I will not allow anyone to harm you or threaten you in any way. You can trust me to protect you." As much as possible, your opening contact should be threat-reducing.

Listening with the Third Ear

There is an expression which is used by mental health workers which describes the process of listening to the message behind a person's communications. It is called "listening with the third ear." It may be commonly referred to as "reading between the lines." In either case, it involves the listener being sensitive to the *real* difficulties which the person may be experiencing even though he may be talking about other issues. In order to accomplish this, the listener does not respond to the small details and minor facts which a person presents, but tries to respond instead to the upset feelings and troubled emotions behind the facts.

For example, a person may say the following: "I'll get those people who have been poisoning my family. I'll take care of them, they won't get me." A "third ear" response to this would be as follows: "You seem angry about the way people are treating you." This avoids a debate between the person and the listener as to who is doing what to whom. The goal of a mental health intervention is not to complete a specific legalistic investigation of the facts. Rather, the goal is to help the person obtain help through the vehicle of your understanding.

Another, less dramatic example occurs when the citizen recites a long history of real difficulties to the officer, such as, "I lost my job, I've been fighting with my wife, I feel sick all the time, etc." Instead of the officer providing specific responses or advice to the individual, such as, "Have you looked at the want ads today?" it would be more effective to indicate that you sense that the person is overwhelmed by all that has been happening to him. This should be shared with the individual in a relaxed, empathic fashion, perhaps using the "reflection of feeling" procedures discussed in Chapter 2.

The officer can pick up cues about what the subject is experiencing from both verbal and non-verbal signs. It is particularly important to do so with feelings of anger, anxiety and mistrust. In providing the individual with your impression of his present feelings, you are not agreeing with any statements which he might be making; rather, you are legitimatizing the feelings which he is experiencing. This differentiation is particularly important when you're dealing with the delusional person who may want others to share his view of the world. Along with responding in the fashion described above, you should attempt to relate to the individual within the following guidelines:

1. Do be sincere, non-threatening and empathic.

2. Do give honest, factual answers whenever necessary.
3. Do not belittle or make fun of any concerns which the subject raises.
4. Do not give the subject advice as to handling his "problems," since they may just be the tip of the iceberg of his emotional disturbance.
5. Do check out your own feelings in response to the subject's statements to insure that your reply is professional, not personal.
6. Do attempt to be supportive in your comments and gestures, as the subject may be feeling very alone.
7. Do not assume that mentally ill people should "know better," and are in need of a good lecturing to straighten themselves out.

If you can communicate the proper understanding to the individual through your listening and active communications, he will become less tense and more responsive to your directions and suggestions for treatment. If there is any "key" to working with mentally disturbed persons, it is being able to listen to their complaints and their frequent tirades without becoming defensive and threatened. Allowing the subject to get his message across to another person who then says, "I understand," is the vehicle which allows the mentally disturbed person to be helped.

Particular Techniques for Specific Problems

Earlier in this chapter, we described a number of specific psychiatric terms and symptoms. The purpose of these descriptions was to assist you in determining the particular problems a person may be experiencing. Once you determine what's wrong, you should have certain techniques at your disposal so you can proceed with effective intervention.

Subject is a compulsive talker. Persons engaged in compulsive talking produce a stream of sometimes meaningless chatter at a rapid, almost non-stop rate. These are understandable communications, but bear little or no relation to the problem at hand. This behavior indicates high levels of anxiety. If your requests to slow down are not effective, you can interrupt the compulsive speech pattern by asking the individual specific concrete questions which he must answer. For example, ask his birth date or address; ask him to give the full name of his children or his parents; ask him where he works or goes to school; or use the other distraction methods described in Chapter 2. Your goal is to interrupt the speech in order to break its pattern and bring it somewhat under control.

Delusional statements. Since delusions were defined as unique ways of viewing the world, delusional statements frequently come into conflict with the views of others. There are three possible responses to delusions:

1. Agree with them.
2. Dispute them.
3. Defer the issue.

If you agree with the mentally disturbed person's delusion, you put yourself in a position of being ineffective in your attempts to provide the person with help. The individual could legitimately ask, "Why do you want me to go to the hospital, since you agree that what I say is true?" Such agreement can also have the effect of increasing the subject's upset state, since the delusion is only a means for him to reduce his anxiety. To have others begin to believe in "his world" may be more frightening than helpful.

The next option, disputing the delusions, is equally ineffective. A direct confrontation with the subject over his disordered thinking may well result in his withdrawing from the person making the attack. He will become inaccessible, or arguments may ensue. This might result in the individual acting-out aggressively due to the threat he experiences.

This leaves the third option, deferring the issue. In this response, the officer does not agree with or dispute the person's statement; rather, he acknowledges the person's view of the world, indicates that it is not his own, and follows with a statement of how he understands the person's feelings. An example of this type of response would be:

Subject: There are many people who want me dead. There is an organization on T.V. which had my name on its list to be executed. I heard them talking about me on T.V.

Officer: I can see you're worried about someone harming you, I don't know of anyone who wants to hurt you, but I really would like to assist you in any way I can to help you feel safer.

In his response, the officer doesn't confirm or dispute the person's view of the world. However, he responds in such a way that the person receives a message of the availability of help.

Subject exhibits paranoid tendencies. Paranoia often involves very severe delusions. You must be very sensitive (both verbally and physically) when you respond to such individuals. Paranoid persons are marked by their extreme suspiciousness and tension. They can appear to be very frightening to others. You must be acutely aware of any indications that the paranoid person is feeling threatened by you. If you detect this fear, you should become as non-threatening as possible, giving the person a feeling that he is in control of the situation. You should neither pick up on any verbal challenge, nor agree that you know anything more about the subject than he tells you. Many paranoid people may say things like, "You know what has been happening to me." Or, "You're a police officer, you have those secret records on me." You must not confirm that you have any special knowledge about the person.

When you're moving into or around a room in which a paranoid person is present, it is a good practice to announce your actions before initiating them. Telling the subject that you are moving across the room to sit in a chair, reduces the probability that he will think you are about to attack him. This telegraphing of your actions assumes that your goal is not to physically subdue the individual.

Subject is conscious but non-responsive. This happens in cases where the person may be catatonic or severely depressed. You should never assume that because a person is not responding to your statements, he is not hearing what you're saying. In these situations there is the temptation to begin acting and talking as if the subject were not present. This is a mistake. Mental illness does not render a person deaf. Therefore, you should make every effort to obtain a response from the individual. This can be done by quietly asking questions and being sensitive to any types of reply, such as a head nod, etc.

If this is not successful, you should attempt to understand the person's thoughts or feelings, and communicate that understanding to him. These "guesses" can be made based on the minimal information which you acquire at the scene, as well as the body posture and emotion the individual may be displaying. By making this effort, you communicate to the subject that you wish to understand his position.

The subject may then feel less threatened about discussing his difficulties with you.

Subject is hallucinatory. Hallucinations are very frightening for the person who is experiencing them. Difficulties emerge when the person is actively hallucinating in the presence of the officer. The first response which you must give is to validate the hallucinatory experience for the individual, but, at the same time, indicate that the hallucination does not (objectively) exist. If an individual is seeing or hearing things, you must indicate that you understand that those experiences are real and frightening for the subject, but that they do not exist in reality. Secondly, you must firmly and empathically indicate that those sensations are due to the extreme emotional stress that the person is experiencing, and that once the stress is lessened, the hallucinations will disappear. You may have to repeat this reassuring message many times, before the individual can begin to respond to it.

Subject is psychotic and aggressive. This is probably the most troublesome situation for any police officer to respond to efficiently. If the subject is in the act of attacking the officer or another individual, there is no question that you should respond with your police control skills. However, in many instances the subject will not be acting out, but will be threatening someone. He may be waving his fists, or a knife, or yelling at you. If the situation is secure, and if no one can be accidentally harmed by the individual, you should adopt a non-threatening, non-confrontative stance with the subject. You may point out that you do not like to get injured or beaten up; that there is no need for the individual to threaten you because you are going to "listen" to him; that getting into a pitched battle with the person may cause more problems than it will solve.

You should then begin talking to the subject as outlined earlier, allowing the individual to vent some of his hostility. You can also indicate this low threat, low offensive style by sitting down, removing your hat, or indulging in similar behaviors. Sit a comfortable distance away from the subject, move the chair so that its back faces the subject, and straddle it. This permits you to use it as a protective block if the person suddenly charges you. It's essential that you appear relaxed and non-threatening, but you must also be on your guard.

These techniques are often very effective in diffusing an otherwise dangerous situation.

The Use of Force in Controlling the Mentally Disturbed Person

Realistically, police are frequently called to intervene in a situation with a disturbed person only after it has deteriorated to the point at which talking is ineffective. The police are often seen as the last resort. The intervention procedures presented thus far assume that the person will at least minimally respond to your comments. However, stalemates can occur between the officers on the scene and the subject. You may have tried repeatedly with every technique available to move the patient from the scene without becoming physically involved. In this situation it may be necessary to respond with a certain amount of physical force to bring the situation to a safe, rapid conclusion.

Physical responses to mentally disturbed people should always be the last resort in any confrontation. When it becomes apparent that physical force is necessary, you should carefully plan what you're going to do before you make your move. There are two alternative forms of action for the situation we've just described.

Subtle physical action. If a patient is quietly but stubbornly refusing to move into a police car, grasping his shoulder firmly and walking him in the direction of the car may be all that is necessary. The following is an actual example of the stalemate situation which I witnessed in an early experience with the local police on a mental health call. It occurred in evaluating a middle-aged woman for hospitalization.

The site was the woman's apartment in a run-down downtown area. I had been talking to her at length about her need for help and the willingness of others to assist. All my persuasive powers were to no avail. At this point, one of the police officers present in the room spotted the woman's purse and hat. He walked over, picked them up, handed them to her saying, "Here, you will be needing these to go outside." After handing the woman the items, he gently but firmly grasped her shoulder and hand to "help her up," and to "insure that she didn't slip as she walked downstairs." She responded without hesitation, arose from the chair and walked out of the door. The officer's intervention was most effective.

If the person is becoming tense, agitated and threatened while refusing to move, a technique like this may not be effective. It may be necessary to totally control the person physically before moving him, in order to avoid injury.

Direct physical action. In the situation where other physical interventions are needed, the guiding principle for the officer should be to have enough manpower available to quickly subdue and overwhelm the individual. Most people, including the mentally disturbed person, will cease to struggle as long as they feel it is hopeless to continue. By using overwhelming force, you reduce the probability of either the subject or the officers being injured. Before acting, you should make the environment as safe as possible, secure your sidearms, and decide among yourselves who will be doing what, e.g., one of you will grab the subject's legs, the other, the left arm, etc. Once you begin acting, you should complete your move as quickly and efficiently as possible, using reasonable force.

After you have subdued the person, you can continue to secure the subject by using cuffs and handholds. Please note: Once the person has been brought under control, don't ignore him. Continue to talk to him, to reassure him that you do not want to harm him and that you still understand that he is having problems. This will reduce his anxiety, as well as his desire to strike out when the cuffs are removed at the hospital.

Outcome and Making the Referral

There are four possible outcomes to any contact with mentally disturbed individuals: The officer can decide that the person is not mentally disturbed and take action through the criminal justice system. He can decide that the person is mentally ill, but that the family members present on the scene will be able to arrange for appropriate psychiatric care. He can decide that the mentally ill person is in need of psychiatric care, and he will arrange a voluntary contact with a mental health service. Or, he can decide that the person is mentally ill and in need of involuntary care and treatment. In each instance, he must take certain actions. We will discuss the last two options since they involve a mental health referral by the officer.

Voluntary committal. In any situation when a referral is appropriate, you should attempt to provide the mental health agency with accurate information. You should contact a professional staff person at the agency, either by phone or in person. In this contact, you should report the reasons why you were called to the scene; what information you collected from family members; any information you obtained from your conversations with the subject; and the apparent cause of the immediate problem. When a subject is sent directly to the psychiatric facility, if you are unable to go with him, it is helpful to have a responsible family member travel to the facility with the subject. This person can then provide some of the information which the staff of the facility may need.

Involuntary committal. If the referral involves involuntary committal, you should attempt to spend some time with the family members discussing the consequences of that disposition. People in general are ignorant of the committal laws and legal aspects of psychiatric admissions in their states. Families which have a member hospitalized involuntarily frequently feel guilty and begin to have doubts and misgivings about their actions. The officer can help these family members by giving them the accurate information they need, and by reassuring them that their decision was appropriate.

Once you've made the referral and it has been acted upon, and the subject has connected with the appropriate mental health resource, your involvement should end. You have completed your duty in discharging your responsibilities in one of the most difficult, complex tasks a modern police officer must face.

References

Bitner, E. Police discretion in emergency apprehension of mentally ill persons. *Social Problems*, 1967, 14, 278-292.

Hollingshead, A.B., & Redlich, F.C. *Social class and mental illness*. New York: John Wiley, 1958.

Liberman, R. Police as a community mental health resource. *Community Mental Health Journal*, 1969, 5, 111-120.

Steadman, H. *Careers of the criminally insane*. New York: D.C. Heath, 1974.

Wender, P. The role of genetics in the etiology of the schizophrenias. *American Journal of Orthopsychiatry*, 1969, 39, 447-458.

5/ Drug and Alcohol Intoxication

Douglas L. Mace

INTRODUCTION

Each year thousands of people are involved in alcohol and drug abuse crisis situations. And you as a police officer will be called on to help the people involved in these crises. What you do and how you react will depend to a large degree upon your knowledge of the area. With this in mind, we are going to examine alcohol and other drug-related crises in order to give you some idea of the types of situations you may be dealing with. We will consider various types of drugs and discuss how they are used and misused, and by which types of people. And, we will discuss the procedures you can use to deal effectively with such crises.

People often have personal definitions of what they mean by "drugs." In recent years when they have talked about drugs, people usually have meant illicit drugs, substances whose possession and use are against the law. Leo Hollister, a pharmacologist at Stanford University, has developed what he calls a social classification of drugs. In his social classification system, however, Hollister talks about which substances actually *are* "drugs" and about why we may see them the way we do. He classifies them into three categories — permissive drugs, prescriptive drugs, and proscriptive drugs — which we will examine next.

TYPES OF DRUGS

Permissive

First, there are the permissive drugs. Permissive drugs are defined as "those substances whose use is socially acceptable." The category includes three major substances: alcohol, caffeine, and nicotine. We don't usually think of caffeine and nicotine as drugs, yet they fit the literal definition of a drug as "a substance which has some physiological effect on the organism." They are also probably the most commonly used drugs in the world (with aspirin possibly a close fourth behind them and alcohol).

Why are they called permissive drugs? Essentially this classification of substances is socially and politically defined, with some economic and moral input. These are the "good" drugs, although we're finally beginning to ask some pointed questions about alcohol. The interesting thing about this definition is its relation — or lack of relation — to the potential harmful effects on the human body, which we'll look at below.

Prescriptive

Prescriptive drugs are those which have a recognized medical usage and, as the term implies, are usually prescribed by a physician for a particular type of medical problem. They are also socially acceptable, but in a carefully defined way.

Proscriptive

Proscriptive drugs are those which are "out" — the "bad" drugs. These include all of the illegal drugs, those substances which we normally have in mind when we discuss drug abuse and drug addiction. Remember, however, that the three types of substances are socially and legally defined. Which category a given substance falls into has very little to do with its actual effect in terms of potential harm to the organism.

For example, statistics from the National Clearinghouse for Smoking and Health indicate that there are 92,000 deaths a year as a result of smoking cigarettes and the nicotine and tars they contain. Leaving out alcohol-related homicides and traffic accidents in which alcohol was a factor, there are 20,000 deaths a year associated with excessive drinking. If you added in the other two categories, some sources say there are another 300,000 deaths that are alcohol-related. If one then looks at some of the drugs which fall into the proscriptive category, marijuana for example, there are no known reported deaths as a direct result of using marijuana. In that instance particularly, then, one certainly cannot say that the substance is proscribed because of its harmful effects on the organism. The categories we put these substances into reflect social, moral, economic and, in some cases, political values much more than they reflect the actual properties of the substances.

The material offered in this chapter was also presented to several groups of police officers undergoing crisis intervention training. The following is a composite of much of the relevant question-and-answer discussion following these talks. We present it here in the hope that many of your questions and concerns will also be answered.

Police Officer: When you say there are no deaths directly linked to use of marijuana, are you making a statement that marijuana in itself is not deadly?

Dr. Mace: Yes, talking about its physical properties and their effects.

Police Officer: Okay. Well I would say that there must be a number of deaths that could be attributed to the use of marijuana starting a chain reaction which induced the person to go on to other drugs. There are a lot of kids who smoke marijuana first. I am of the school that says that that starts it and that it doesn't end with marijuana.

Dr. Mace: Most people who have worked with drug-dependent individuals in any depth don't subscribe to what is generally called the "stepping-stone" theory of drug dependence. No drug, in and of itself — even those with the highest potential for addiction like morphine or some of the other opiates, or cocaine which supposedly has an extremely high potential for psychological dependency — no drug in and of itself forces anybody to continue using it. It may lay some groundwork in terms of producing effects that are pleasurable to the individual — effects that he wants to experience again. In that sense, any substance that changes the consciousness of the individual, which alters his way of perceiving things and the way that he feels, is going to have the potential for getting that individual to want to use it again.

Police Officer: You're talking about psychologically?

Dr. Mace: Psychologically — right, not physiologically. If you start talking about that then you can make no distinction whatsoever, for example, between marijuana and alcohol. And there are far more people involved with alcohol in terms of excessive usage. The last figure I saw is something like 9,000,000 excessive drinkers in this country.

Police Officer: If marijuana were made legal, do you think it would follow the same course that alcohol has?

Dr. Mace: No.

Police Officer: Well, look at it this way, one reason you've got the 9,000,000 alcoholics is because it's legal. If it wasn't quite as accessible you'd have a lot of people — your borderline people — who wouldn't be doing it.

Dr. Mace: It would be very interesting to look at the percentage of the population who were excessive drinkers or alcoholics during Prohibition. My own bias is that the way to control the use of any substance is not through its legality or illegality. That doesn't mean that I'm in favor of legalizing all substances. Rather, from the point of view of long-term change in patterns of drug usage by the society and by individuals, I feel that you will never change those patterns to any significant degree for any length of time simply by making a substance legal or illegal. Prohibition certainly proved that.

Another issue concerning the degree of criminality of marijuana is the question of just how harmful it would be as a legalized drug. Would it really be all that harmful if we decriminalized it? I think not. Look at the percentage of law enforcement time that may be involved in dealing with the social marijuana user or simple possessor of marijuana; the percentage of criminal court time; the diversion of both kinds of resources to the enforcement of the marijuana laws. Then look at the social effects on the convicted possessor of marijuana who may never be involved in any other kind of illegal activity, and particularly the long-term social effects of possession being a felony.

When you start examining the social cost-effectiveness of marijuana laws and get away from the ethical, moral and social values and all the mythology that has built up around marijuana, there is good reason to support the idea of at least decriminalizing this particular substance. When you also consider the potential for harmful effect to the individual, this illegal substance is considerably less harmful than alcohol, and it's probably less harmful than nicotine, both of which are not only legal but whose use is actively promoted.

Police Officer: What about all these studies that have shown that there is genetic damage not only in the generation that it's used in, but the following generations also. I've read many articles that say they have linked marijuana with genetic damage.

Dr. Mace: I would advise anybody who is seriously interested in pursuing the question of the harmful effects of marijuana to take a look at the March, 1975 issue of *Consumer Reports* and the book that was also put out by *Consumer Reports* a couple of years ago, *Licit and Illicit Drugs,* an excellent source book for the whole area of drugs, including alcohol. The *Consumer Reports* article did a very effective job of presenting both sides of the research that has been done, of taking a close look from a scientific point of view. The article looks at the design of the research, the way they go about selecting the people who are included in the study, the kinds of things they do in the research, and the way their findings are then reported. There's never been any major study that has reported severe or even moderately harmful effects of marijuana that has been able to be reproduced by anyone else.

Police Officer: Most of us, I believe, in the police department feel it should be decriminalized. I do anyway. There should be some kind of a restriction on sales, of course, but I can't see putting a kid in jail for smoking marijuana. I think we're more interested in youth than the smoking of marijuana. In order to get marijuana you're gonna have to go to the drug-oriented society. You don't just go to the drugstore and buy three joints. The fact that you're introduced into that society is going to be a bad influence number one; they're not gonna stop at marijuana — I think anybody here that has anything to do with drugs — every kid we've ever talked to — he didn't start shooting up heroin, he started smoking grass. So how can you talk about making it more available?

Dr. Mace: I think that you partially answered that objection yourself when you said that at least as things currently stand, with marijuana's status as a proscriptive drug, the likelihood is very high that the same guy who is dealing marijuana is also dealing in pills and in cocaine and maybe in heroin; and that certainly increases the likelihood — particularly since the profit margin for the dealer is higher on those substances — that he is going to push those drugs to the individual. Of course, you may at least partly avoid exposing the individual to harder drugs by decriminalizing or legalizing marijuana and making it unprofitable for the hard drug dealer to handle.

Police Officer: If you decriminalize, or legalize marijuana, won't that make the dealers more likely to turn kids on to something harder?

Dr. Mace: There are basically two categories of people who sell marijuana: the people who don't sell anything else and are informal dealers for a network of their friends and acquaintances; and the multi-drug dealer who is involved in selling a variety of other substances. The likelihood is that legalizing it (particularly if in legalizing it you set up a system of distribution similar to the one that exists for liquor in this country) would have two effects. The casual dealer who's dealing only marijuana may get hurt because he wasn't particularly interested in dealing any other drug. He was doing a favor for friends, sort of like the neighborhood liquor dealer during Prohibition. The guy who's dealing hard drugs, on the other hand, is simply going to drop this from his inventory because it doesn't sell, people can get it easier some place else.

Police Officer: He's going to lose his contact with the people who only smoke marijuana.

Dr. Mace: That's right. We get back to the idea of exposure. If you accept the idea that one of the reasons that people who start out on marijuana may go on to harder drugs is that they get it from the guy who's dealing both in some instances.

TYPES OF DRUG USE

There are four categories of drug-taking: use, misuse, dependence, and addiction. Very often, just as we tend to talk about different types of drugs as but a single category, we also tend to use all of these drug-taking terms as meaning the same thing when, in fact, they mean very different things.

Use

One can talk about *use* of literally any substance, whichever classification of drugs it falls into. Use can mean either taking a prescriptive drug in the manner in which it was prescribed or infrequently or very moderately taking any other substance in ways which do not pose any physical danger for the individual, and do not interfere with his ability to function effectively. Use means that the substance does not take the place of an individual's personal resources in dealing with feelings, with other people or with life situations.

One researcher discovered a group of people who apparently are users of heroin, but who are not physically addicted to it, nor do they depend on it on any regular basis for dealing with reality. Once a month or so they shoot up because they like the effects. It's apparently sort of like somebody going to a cocktail party once every month and having a few drinks. People generally don't think this is possible with heroin; either you're an out-and-out addict or you don't touch the stuff at all.

One can also talk about users of alcohol; for example, the person who has an occasional drink, or stops at a bar on his way home and has a beer. His drug-taking (alcohol) is in a social context, it doesn't interfere particularly with his functioning, and has no long-term effects on him, his family or his ability to work effectively. That's use of a substance.

Misuse

Misuse of a substance means either taking some kind of substance inappropriately (particularly in terms of prescribed medication), or substituting a substance for the ability to cope with a situation or deal with it by using your own resources. For example, the person who feels he *has* to stop and have a couple of drinks before he does something that he's not used to doing, like speaking in front of a group of people, is misusing alcohol. If he's substituting the effect of the alcohol for his self-confidence then in essence he's misusing that substance. If his misuse is consistent enough he may become dependent on the substance.

Or, take the person who is suffering from a loss in his family and goes to the family physician and the physician says, "I know you're really upset, let me give you a prescription for a tranquilizer — Librium." The person takes the prescription, has it filled, sticks it in the medicine cabinet and may use it for two or three days until he has calmed down. He keeps it in the medicine cabinet and at some future time, without ever returning to the doctor to see if it's still indicated for some new situation, starts to get anxious again and says, "Well, I'll go take a couple of the Librium." This, by definition, is misuse. Or, the individual who has a medication prescribed that is to be taken one tablet three times a day, and decides that that's not having the effect that he feels it ought to have, so he takes two, three times a day. That is misuse. Another kind of misuse is the kid who's experimenting with drugs, who takes acid a couple of times because he wants to find out "who he really is."

Dependence

We can talk about *dependence*, defined as "frequent or consistent taking of some substance because it gives the individual the feeling of being able to function better." This is the realm in which most of the serious drug problems fall, regardless of what kind of substance is involved. Even in the case of caffeine, alcohol, nicotine and all the other permissive drugs, any such behavior, particularly when it gets to the point both of substituting for some other kinds of more appropriate behavior, and when it interferes with the individual's functioning, is dependence. We can talk about dependence on any drug substance.

Addiction

Addiction has a very specific medical meaning. To be considered addictive, a substance must meet two criteria: first, using the substance produces a tolerance to its effects so that in order to maintain the same effect, the person has to increase the dosage; and second, when one stops using it, there will be definite withdrawal symptoms. Addiction means a physical dependence on the drug involved. The primary categories of addictive drugs are heroin, the other opiates, and the barbiturates.

TYPES OF DRUG USERS

Adolescents

One important drug user group is adolescents. We have looked at some of the reasons why adolescents shouldn't use drugs. But why do they often do so? The adolescent is concerned with his identity, he is somebody who is trying to find out "who he is." He may see it as very desirable to have a quick and easy way of doing this. Thus, the hallucinogenic drugs may be very attractive to teenagers, since they are supposed to provide self-awareness, allowing the person to expand his consciousness, to learn about what's going on inside himself. Obviously, this is a poor way to go about it, partly because many things other than self-awareness enter into the drug experience with the hallucinogens. Also, depending on his level of development, he may be panicked by the sudden flood of internal stimulation and the feeling that he is completely out of control that often take place under some of the hallucinogens.

Another reason adolescents take drugs includes thrill-seeking, a feeling of wanting to experience new things that are exciting. A final reason for adolescent drug use is that parents, society, school officials and other adult figures have said that this is something one shouldn't do; and adolescents in some instances are ready to do anything that's anti-authority. This may have been more likely to happen in the days when scare drug education was popular and most of the people doing drug education, including most of the professionals, knew less about what they were talking about in terms of drug effects than the kids to whom they were talking.

Middle-Aged Group

Another category of people who are likely to misuse or be dependent upon drugs are people in the 36 to 55 age range, particularly women who have never held jobs and who are primarily housewives. They are likely to use substances and eventually become dependent upon them out of boredom, loneliness or a feeling of lack of self-worth. The use of drugs is specifically designed to make them feel better — to give them an internal feeling of calm and comfort. Using barbiturates and amphetamines in this group, particularly diet pills and/or sleeping pills, is heavy.

Dependency-Prone

A third important type of drug user is the dependency-prone person. This is an individual who has difficulty in coping with his feelings, in being able to identify them, being able to say, "It's okay to feel depressed sometimes — it's an ordinary sort of thing." If he feels depressed, to him that means there's something wrong. If he feels anxious, it means there's something wrong. He hasn't developed the skills necessary to deal with ordinary cycles of emotion. He also has a tendency to see things as primarily happening outside of himself. He doesn't believe he really has much influence on what happens to him; but, instead, it is the external world that really guides him.

Because of his lack of coping skills and his external orientation this person has the tendency to look for external solutions. Among the external solutions are any substances which change the way he feels and make him feel better able to cope with the realities of the outside world. When he discovers such substances he starts using them frequently because they give him the impression of being able to deal more effectively with things. This is the point at which one gets into a real dependency. It can happen with almost any kind of substance.

DRUG CRISES

Medical

Let's look at the types of crises that may evolve out of drug misuse, dependence or addiction. These are relatively limited in number and in the types of interventions that are necessary. The first category is the medical crisis. These are situations in which medical intervention is the primary element. The police officer may be involved as the first person notified or the first person who arrives on the scene.

Overdose. There are two basic categories of medical crisis. The first is the overdose, which can occur with heroin, barbiturates, tranquilizers or alcohol. Usually in these situations you will be dealing with an individual who is comatose or extremely drowsy, who may have some history of prior drug usage, or near whom you may find some evidence that he has been taking drugs; for example, a hypodermic needle or pill bottle. In this situation the only appropriate intervention is to get the person to medical treatment as rapidly as possible. Quick attention is essential.

The most critical situation is one involving an individual who has taken a combination of barbiturates and alcohol, or tranquilizers and alcohol. In this instance you are not dealing with the effects of the two added together, but a multiplication of effects, so that the critical time period in getting that individual to help is a lot shorter than it would be if he had taken a single drug. Most likely the only way you're going to know if somebody has taken both alcohol and drugs will be from physical evidence (e.g., pills, medication or liquor bottles), or a history obtained from people around him. There is almost no way to determine if someone has taken a combination simply by examining the individual. So, if you suspect anything like that, you should raise the question of multiple drugs, or at least keep it in mind.

Withdrawal. The other medical crisis that occurs is withdrawal. There are two basic types of drug withdrawal, with different degrees of severity. The first occurs with alcohol, barbiturates, and with some tranquilizers. With these, withdrawal usually takes place within 24 to 48 hours after the individual stops heavy and consistent use. If the individual doesn't receive medical attention within a few hours after the withdrawal symptoms begin, he has a high potential for going into cardiac failure and dying. In barbiturate and alcohol withdrawal there is also a high potential for convulsions. As with overdose, the appropriate intervention is to get medical help as quickly as possible.

The second type of withdrawal occurs with heroin. Here, and with some of the other opiates, the situation is not as life-threatening as with the first group of substances. In fact, in most instances, withdrawal from even a heavy heroin habit is not life-threatening at all, although it may be extremely unpleasant for the individual. It is certainly desirable to get medical assistance, but it's not as urgent as it is with the individual whom you suspect is in withdrawal from alcohol, the barbiturates and some tranquilizers.

Psychiatric

The second major category of crisis is the psychiatric crisis. The psychiatric crisis is a crisis resulting from drugs, but resembling a psychotic episode with no drug involvement. The psychiatric crisis occurs in the individual who is having a bad trip on one of the hallucinogens — LSD, STP, PCP, etc. He is someone who is extremely panicked. A bad trip usually occurs in someone who has taken a drug which produces some very unpleasant effects, or in the unstable individual who is not too well put together to start with and now has all kinds of strange things going on in his head as a result of the drug.

He is absolutely petrified of what's going on within him. He may be talking about extremely strange things, about seeing things in a peculiar way, about perceiving people as changing shapes in front of his eyes, or about faces melting and changing into something else. He may talk about strange sensations in relation to the environment, such as seeing the walls move or go in and out, as if the room was breathing. He may talk about feeling like the floor is moving under him. All of these bizarre-sounding things should allow you to identify this person as somebody who is probably either psychotic or having a bad trip.

Intervening in this situation is similar to dealing with the psychotic individual. You need to approach the person calmly, in a way that is non-threatening and isn't going to contribute to his panic. Keep in mind, especially, that you may be dealing with someone who fears police officers. It may seem to him that all of a sudden two officers are changing into a hundred storm troopers coming into his apartment. It is especially important to approach him very calmly, and reassure him that he's going to be all right, that you are there for his protection and to help him. It's also desirable, if there is a lot of noise, a lot of movement, or a lot of people around, to try to reduce the level of stimulation as much as possible.

The individual who is having a bad trip, or even the individual who is having a good trip, is somebody who is very sensitive to changes and to any kind of stimulation in the environment. The traditional crisis center for people on bad trips usually was a place that was dimly-lighted, comfortably furnished and away from any kind of noise — a very comfortable, reassuring, restful kind of place. The primary danger in this kind of situation is probably not that the individual is going to attack somebody; but rather, that because of his panic he will inadvertently hurt himself or someone else. He may try to get away from something that is terrifying him. He may jump out a window because he doesn't know it's a window, or because it seems to him that jumping through it is more desirable than being attacked by the monsters he sees in front of him. If there is some indication that he is a danger either to himself or to other people around, you will want to restrain the individual. The primary idea should be to bring the individual under control so that he won't hurt himself, and at the same time try to reduce his panic by being reassuring, and restraining him as you might a panicked child.

The second step in dealing with this kind of individual, ideally, is referral to a drug crisis center. If none is available, a less desirable alternative is the hospital emergency room. Unfortunately, unless the hospital has considerable experience with such cases, it may make the situation worse. The atmosphere may increase the individual's panic, and treatment with anything other than Valium or Librium may produce serious reactions and even death.

One other type of psychiatric crisis may involve the individual who shows all of the symptoms of a bad trip but gives no evidence that he has recently taken a drug. In this instance you may be dealing with an individual who's having a flashback from some previous bad trip and is actually reliving much of that trip. The intervention with somebody who is having a flashback is the same as with somebody having a bad trip.

Situational

The final class of crisis — the situational crisis — includes two types of individuals, the amphetamine user and the person who is intoxicated. People in the medical, psychiatric and law enforcement fields talk about three major categories of dangerous drugs — alcohol, cocaine and the amphetamines — from the point of view of how dangerous the individual who uses them is. Particularly in the case of amphetamine or cocaine users, you are dealing with people who are extremely dangerous. This kind of individual will be very jumpy, very reactive to things, unable to keep still. He may be wringing his hands, talking very fast, talking about a lot of different things, talking about people having followed him, and chain-smoking. If he is a long-term user of amphetamines he may be very drawn and emaciated. He may be extremely suspicious of everything that is going on around him. He may lick his lips frequently, since one of the side effects of amphetamine use is extreme dryness of the mouth and lips.

This person is very dangerous. He's somebody you should never let out of your sight, and never turn your back on. The primary intervention is to immobilize the individual as soon as possible. If you don't, it is quite likely that someone will get hurt. Immobilizing him should be undertaken with the recognition that:

1. He's going to be very quick.
2. He's going to be very strong.
3. He's going to be out to defend himself in every way that he conceivably can.

Immobilizing him is probably going to take more officers than one would suspect it should. There is relatively little need for the kinds of reassurance and gentleness that you might want to exercise with the person on a bad trip.

Finally, in dealing with an intoxicated individual, you should keep in mind the fact that anybody who has been consuming substantial amounts of alcohol often shows an increase in irritability in response to other people's behavior toward him. Some suggestions for handling this individual deal with listening to the way you're communicating with him. What tone of voice are you using? How is he likely to interpret the tone? What should your choice of words be? Will they be perceived as threatening? Further, given that this is an individual who is highly irritable and reactive, and is likely to be belligerent and insulting, the person trying to deal with him should try to avoid reacting to these things as if it were coming from somebody who is completely sober and in full possession of his faculties.

In this chapter we have presented some of the very basic facts about drug and alcohol abuse; and have reviewed some related crisis situations which you will be faced with in your career as a police officer. However, this by no means covers the wide variety of situations you will encounter. It will, nevertheless, give you a working knowledge of the related problems you'll deal with in this area.

6/ Rape

Agnes Harrington
Karen Sutton-Simon

Rape is one of the most frequently committed violent crimes in the United States today. In 1974 alone more than 55,000 rapes were recorded by law enforcement officials, and subsequent years have been worse. However, experts estimate that the actual number may be much higher, since a great many cases are never reported. Even worse, it appears that rape is on the rise. Reports have shown a 49% increase since 1969. Undoubtedly, rape is a major problem for law enforcement personnel, and the problem seems to be growing.

Despite its frequency and our concern over this type of crime, we know very little about rape or the men who commit it. Until recently, many rape victims were too ashamed to report their attack. Even when they did contact the police, many victims were too confused or upset in the aftermath of the attack to provide police and researchers with useful information. Against this background of shame and confusion it has been extremely difficult to learn about rape. It is, thus, not surprising that this particular crime is surrounded by as many myths as facts.

Recently, this situation has started to change. From police, researchers and rape victims we have begun to collect information which can help us understand the crime, its perpetrators and its victims. It is the purpose of this chapter to explore the facts of rape and provide procedural information for the police officer who must respond to such crisis calls.

FACTS AND MYTHS ABOUT RAPE

Rape — The Crime

When we hear of a rape, our first thought is that a sex crime has been committed. Most people believe that the primary motive behind rape is sexual. This is questioned, however, by law enforcement personnel and researchers because one quality of the crime stands out above all others — aggression. Nonphysical force, such as the threat of bodily injury or the threat of injury with a weapon, is used in 87% of all rapes. Physical force, such as beating, roughness and choking, is used in 85% of all rapes. The aggression often continues even after the victim has been forced into submission. At least 15% of all rapists beat, choke and kick their victims during and after the rape. In the rare case when aggression is not part of the incident, the victims are usually much younger than their attackers. It seems that almost the only non-violent rapes are committed by older men against young girls.

Other information supports this idea of rape as a crime of violence. Studies show that many rapists are men who have normal sex lives and who could find other sexual outlets. It seems that one of the reasons they rape women instead, is because of the extra ingredient in a rape — the aggression against the victim. Rape fully deserves its classification as a crime of violence.

One of the myths surrounding rape is that it is a spontaneous act and occurs only when a man's sexual impulses get out of control. The popular picture of the rapist is a man who is driven to rape by his uncontrollable sex drive. This picture is rarely true. In 71% of all cases, the attack is premeditated and planned. Prior to the act, the rapist has decided he will have sexual relations and he has either picked out his victim or has chosen a location to wait for the first likely female. Part of the rapist's plan will include the situation he will construct to trap his victim. Thus, at least 71% of all rapes are not spontaneous crimes of passion.

Another 11% are partially planned. These rapes occur when a man realizes that a woman is in a vulnerable position and he decides to take advantage of it. His plan to rape the woman is made only after he has encountered her and sees that the situation is "ripe" for an attack. In the rare case when rape is unplanned or "explosive," it often occurs after the rapist has committed another felony. "Explosive" rapes are frequently of the "since you've robbed her, you might as well rape her" variety. Almost every rape committed by two or more men against the same woman is premeditated.

In the minds of many of us, rape is a crime that takes place in the dark of night on a dead-end street. This picture is only partly correct. Eleven percent of all rapes do take place out of doors – in parking lots, school yards and parks – and 71% of all rapes take place between 8:00 p.m. and 8:00 a.m. However, far more often, rape is an indoor event and sometimes, it occurs in broad daylight. Sixty-seven percent of all rapes occur indoors and 29% take place between 8:00 a.m. and 8:00 p.m. Women are raped in laundry rooms, vacant buildings and even their own homes.

The Rapist

Criminologists, psychologists and other researchers have worked to figure out what type of person commits rape and what his motives are. These experts have had some success in answering such questions, but they have also discovered that it is extremely difficult to characterize and understand the "typical" rapist. Studies of rapists show that the kind of men who commit this crime are so different from each other that they almost defy general description. In addition, the rapist's motives are more puzzling to us than other felons' motives. To begin to understand who the rapist is and what leads him to rape, we will review the work of various researchers. It is important to remember that we have only recently begun to study the rapist. There is much information missing and, at this time, we have for the most part only theories and guesses. Firm conclusions about the rapist and his motives must await further research.

If we had to draw a picture of the "typical" rapist, he would be between 15 and 25 years old, single, and from a lower class background. He would be unemployed or working as a laborer. However, since 3.6% of all rapes are committed by boys younger than 15, and 3.6% by men on the far side of 40, we know that rapists can be any age. In addition, 17% of all rapists are married and many hold white-collar or professional jobs. In many cases, rapists are just like the guy next door – a family man holding down a steady job.

One of the myths of rape suggests that black men rape white

women. Recent figures show that this is not the case. Rather, it seems that black men rape black women and white men rape white women. Black women are victims in 96% of all rapes committed by black men, and white women are victims of 82% of all rapes committed by white men. For whatever reasons, rape is an intraracial rather than an interracial affair.

Most rapists have prior arrest records, often dating back to their adolescence. Even though we know that most rapists are repeated offenders, less than 10% have previous arrest records for rape. Only 4% of men charged with rape have arrest records for such sex offenses as exhibitionism. This indicates that most rapists are not involved in previous sex crimes.

We generally think that the rapist chooses a stranger at random as his victim. This is true in about 42% of all rapes. However, rape, like murder, often takes place between people who know each other. In 24% of all cases, the victims report that they recognized their attacker by sight or considered him an acquaintance. In 33%, the victims report that their attacker was an ex-boyfriend, an old family friend, a neighbor or a relative. The message behind these statistics is that rape is a possibility between any man and woman, regardless of the relationship.

Let's consider the mind and personal life of the rapist to see if we can find any clues to what leads him to rape. Again, we must remember that we are working with hypotheses — scientific guesses — and we must still wait for further research. In the movies and on T.V., the rapist is frequently portrayed as a weird-looking, disturbed man. This image of the rapist rarely matches reality because the surprising fact is that most rapists are psychologically quite normal. Psychological studies, tests and interviews show that the personalities of rapists are no different from those of other men, and aside from their committing rape, their sexual adjustment is often quite good. The major difference between the rapist and the guy next door is that the rapist tends to be more violent. He is a man with a great deal of anger who is capable of exploding into a rage.

If rapists are, in general, quite normal, how can we account for their single abnormality? This is the real question and a number of answers have been proposed. Some writers, particularly women, see the male-dominated society as a breeding ground for rapists. They suggest that in a society which prizes the John Wayne brand of masculinity where all men are strong, level-headed and dominant, rapists are men who have carried these qualities too far. Strong becomes brutal, level-headed becomes uncaring, and dominant becomes overpowering. These writers suggest that some men overdo their masculinity and display it by overpowering women against their will.

Some women have also suggested that rape may be the outcome of the way our society views sex. These writers maintain that in our society, sex is a commodity and a woman is part of the sale. Men feel they have to buy sex, either directly as through a prostitute, or indirectly as through courtship and marriage. When sex is something that must be purchased, these writers suggest, all men are looking for a bargain. The cheapest bargain of all is rape; the sex is free and the consequences are few. While such writers have made us aware of the feelings of many women, it seems difficult to blame rape on a male-dominated society. Not every man is a rapist, yet all come from the same society.

One theory, called the "double-standard" theory, suggests that rapists have had unusually close relationships with their mothers in childhood. These men do not just love their mothers, they idolize them and put them on pedestals. As adults, these men compare all women to their idolized mothers. Most women fail to measure up to the perfect picture. These men then develop contempt and hatred for all women, which easily turn to rage. Their motive for raping women is to vent this rage, to hurt and humiliate women. At the same time, these men express very moral feelings about "good" women; that is, women they think are like their perfect mothers. Unfortunately, no woman alive can ever match this fantasy.

Although studies show that the sexual adjustment of the majority of rapists is good, there are some men who seem to commit rape because of their own sexual problems. These are the rapists who are also convicted of sex crimes. It is suggested that these men commit rape because they are unable to have normal heterosexual relationships. They feel sexually inadequate and impotent. They compensate for these feelings by acting in a super-masculine way. Rape is their means to prove that they are really men.

Anger and aggression are consistent themes in the study of rape. Psychologists believe that for one group of rapists, aggression is the sole motive behind the attack. These men commit what experts call "assaultive" rapes and are violent and hostile men. They can only relieve their pent-up anger through sexual assault. They are sadistic rapists who beat their victims even when the use of force is unnecessary to commit the rape. These men just seem to enjoy beating women.

Obviously, any man who commits rape does not think highly of women. Psychologists have suggested that one group of rapists does not even see them as people. These men are supposedly unable to love or feel close to any other person, man or woman. They are only concerned with themselves and their own sexual satisfaction. If they want sexual satisfaction, they take it without asking; after all, only their pleasure matters.

When rape is committed by a man who is otherwise unknown to the police, who has no history of violence or sexual problems, the motive behind the rape is especially confusing. Psychologists have found that in many cases, such men commit the crime after a bout of heavy drinking or when out on the town with the boys. It seems that when drunk or raising hell, some men set aside their consciences and moral convictions and commit rape, something they would never do if sober or by themselves. These theories of why men commit rape provide an idea of the way psychologists view the rapist's mind. We can conclude that the motives behind rape are almost as different as the men who commit them.

The Victim of Rape

Two great myths have hounded the victims of rape since biblical times. The first myth suggests that women who get raped are asking for it. The second myth suggests that any woman, if she really wants to, can prevent a rape. Not only are these ideas fictitious, but they are also harmful to the victims, and have caused them untold suffering. Let us examine some of the facts about rape victims in order to put these myths to rest.

There are records that infants as young as six months and women as old as 93 have been raped. Were these victims asking to be raped? Of course not. But, you may say, these are highly unusual cases, the work of rapists who are insane. Such victims are unusual, but we mention them to make a point: women of all ages are raped, not just young attractive ones. Statistics show that in 28% of all rapes the victims are girls under 14, and in 10%, the victims are women over 40.

It is difficult to believe that this large group of victims is asking to be raped.

But what about women between 14 and 40? Presumably, these are women with greater sexual interests. How do we know that they are not looking for the opportunity to be raped? A number of facts help to dispel this myth. For many rape victims, the assault occurs during the course of their daily routine. Women are raped in apartment house laundry rooms, in parking lots after work and while asleep in their own beds. In all these situations, the women are not out looking for action; but rather the men are out looking for the women.

The idea that most women can physically prevent a rape if they want to seems difficult to support. Many women do try. But, you will recall, force or the threat of injury is a factor in about 87% of all cases. Forty-five percent of all rape victims do resist their attackers. In a survey of women who had been raped, 27% reported that they screamed, and tried to escape; 18% kicked, fought and threw things at their assailant. Many women used more than one form of resistance. Perhaps the only ways in which a woman could be certain she could prevent being raped are by never being alone, and by being an expert in karate. Thus, the two myths can be put to rest — women neither ask to be raped nor are they usually able to prevent it when it does occur.

THE AFTERMATH OF RAPE

Let us consider the condition of the rape victim after the assault, and the changes in her life that follow the crime. The emotional reaction of women immediately after being raped is unpredictable. Some women are hysterical and cannot make sense to the responding officers. Other women are surprisingly composed and seem to have their wits about them. Still others may be in a traumatic daze. None of these reactions is unusual to any form of extreme stress. All require patience and understanding on the part of police personnel.

Physical Problems

The stresses of rape do not end for the victim once her attacker is finished with her. Almost every rape victim experiences physical and emotional problems after she has been raped. The physical problems must be dealt with first. There are the possibilities of pregnancy and VD, and the need for treatment for injuries sustained during the attack. When the woman reports the rape to the police, she must undergo the required medical exam for evidence. So soon after the attack, this exam may be very painful.

Emotional Problems

The emotional problems come later but, as rape victims report, they are no less painful than the physical ones. Many victims experience uncontrollable terror long after the rape. These woman are afraid to be alone, and they awake in the night in the grips of harrowing nightmares. These fears disrupt the rape victim's life. Sometimes the fear leaves her unable to return to normal sexual relations. Many rape victims report that they are terrified of all men, are afraid of being killed or are disgusted by any sexual activity.

Some of the emotional problems that these victims face involve friends and family. It is not unusual for rape victims to report that their husband's attitude toward them changed. Some husbands have no sympathy for their wives and see the rape as unimportant. Others see their wives as dirty, defiled women and want nothing to do with them. Some husbands urge their wives not to report the attack or to drop charges because they, the husbands, would be humiliated.

Perhaps the most lasting and damaging of all the problems that a rape victim faces are those that appear within her own thoughts. The rape victim often experiences guilt, shame, embarrassment, anger and a sense of worthlessness. She sees herself as a degraded woman whom no one could love or care about. The rape victim, too, has bought the myths of rape and endlessly asks herself, "How could I have prevented it? What did I do to provoke him?" It is impossible to guess how deep these scars go or how badly they disrupt a woman's life. The only sign we have of the rape victim's private suffering is the frequent statement, "I would rather be killed than survive another rape."

In this section, we have reviewed some of the significant facts about rape. The major task of police personnel still lies ahead: dealing with the victims of rape and investigating this type of crime. In the section that follows, we will review police procedure relevant to rape.

THE ROLE OF THE POLICE IN A CASE OF RAPE

As police officers, one of our most difficult tasks is handling rape cases. Our procedures for dealing with the victim and investigating the crime are complex and unlike those for other crimes. In addition, the nature of rape makes the report and investigation uncomfortable for both the officers and the victims. Recently, we in police work have been asked about the investigation and prevention of rape by a concerned public. For all these reasons, it is vitally important that we be thoroughly familiar with rape report and investigation procedures. In this section we'll review the procedures involved in rape cases and consider some ways to prevent the crime. The more we know about rape and the police officer's duties on this type of case, the more effectively will we be able to carry out our jobs and prevent future rapes.

Working with the Victim of Rape

We know that many rapes go unreported, which allows the rapist the opportunity to attack other victims. When we ask women why they do not report rapes, one of the answers we frequently hear is, "I couldn't go through the police investigation." Whether or not this reaction is justified, it tells us that as police officers, we must take a good look at how we work with the victims of rape. Most of us experience compassion for the victim; yet, compassion alone is not enough. During our investigation, we must offer support and guidance and sometimes, advice. Let us consider what we can and must do.

The first responsibility of any officer on a rape case is to create an atmosphere of trust for the victim. This can be done by the way the officer acts while taking the initial report. Even though the initial report is a routine job for the area officer or the detective/investigator, it is not a routine experience for the victim. We must keep in mind that the rape victim has just suffered the most humiliating experience of her life. She will be upset and in need of support. We police officers can offer this support while taking the initial report by remaining calm and official, yet warm and understanding. We can try to help the victim recall the facts of the rape; but we should avoid unnecessary questioning.

Procedure. We can also aid the victim by providing her with clear instructions about the procedure that will follow. In New York and many other states, the victim should first be informed not to bathe and to keep her outer garments and underclothing for laboratory examination. She should also be told that she will be required to undergo a medical exam for evidence of rape. The officer should make sure to tell her that no police will be present during the examination. Many women mistakenly believe an officer must be present in the examination room. If the victim is a juvenile, the officer must also obtain parental permission for the hospital examination.

Once the initial report is completed, the officer must then determine whether or not the victim wishes to prosecute. Throughout all the questioning, we must remember that it is embarrassing for the victim to talk to a male investigator. While you can help ease this embarrassment by the way you conduct yourselves, you should also let the victim know that if she prefers, and if one is available,[1] a female officer will be present, take affidavit and assist the victim in any way she can. When the initial report has been taken, the officer must transport the victim to the hospital for the exam. When the hospital releases the victim, her contact with the police will continue until the conclusion of the investigation and the referral of the case to the District Attorney.

In some cases of rape, the area officer or CID investigator may believe that the victim was too easy a target for rape because of her own actions. Sometimes you may feel that a woman brought the rape upon herself. No woman asks for rape but because many believe that "it could never happen to me," they take unnecessary chances. Even though you may feel that a rape could have been avoided, as police officers, you must never let your thoughts or feelings surface. You must never judge the victim, but remember that you are dealing with a human being who is suffering.

When the victim is brought to the precinct for the conclusion of the investigation, she should be made as comfortable as possible. Further questioning and taking the affidavit should be done as far away from other personnel as possible. Although only the investigator concerned knows that this woman has been raped, the victim feels that

---

[1] There are a growing number of states in which the presence of a female officer during this investigation is automatic, and occurs in all such rape investigations.

everyone knows and is looking at her. She experiences the stigma of rape that the officer should help ease.

Most rape victims will have many questions about police procedure. Be prepared to answer all questions, especially those about the "line-up," which rape victims often find very frightening. Often, victims will want to know what will happen once the suspect is apprehended. Calm her fears by telling her that all questions relative to court procedure will be explained to her by the District Attorney's office. Assure her that the D.A.'s staff will go over all the details with her.

The rape victim continues to suffer even after the rape itself. She may need counseling, and the police can help her find the appropriate agency. Police departments should maintain a list of referral agencies which provide counseling for the rape victim and her family. Have your agency list ready for her; but be sure that you've checked with the agencies and that they are ready to help her. Some of our larger cities have agencies which also offer help to the husband and parents of the rape victim. In our eagerness to investigate and apprehend, let us not forget the feelings and emotions of the victim of rape. She has lived through an ordeal but has a future to face. We, as police officers, can help her face that future.

The Investigation

The original report of a rape is usually taken by the area officer. At this time, the victim may be upset or in a state of shock. For this reason, all the officer's questions must be brief and to the point. Your first task is to determine who the suspect is. If the victim does not know the suspect, obtain a description so that a general message can be immediately put on the air. The area officer should next contact his investigative office so that an investigator will be assigned to the case. The area officer should then advise the victim of the immediate procedure she should follow, and then transport her to the hospital where she will be examined and treated by a hospital physician, a police physician, or if she prefers, her personal physician.

It is important that police officers be familiar with emergency room procedures for rape victims. There is often a delay and sometimes a lengthy wait until the victim is examined. It may seem as though hospital personnel are unconcerned about the victim. This is usually far from true, and they will attend to her as soon as they are able. Hospital personnel also have procedures which they must follow. Recently, many nurses have received special training in working with rape victims and have learned what to record on the victim's chart for possible court use. In this way, both hospital and police personnel are seeking to keep the rape victim their first concern.

When the victim is released from the hospital, if she agrees to prosecute, she will be taken to headquarters, where her affidavit will be taken. The victim should be advised that a female officer will take her affidavit if she prefers to talk to a woman. Before taking her statement, the investigator should discuss with her what is needed in an affidavit. A lengthy affidavit is not always the best one. The best procedure is to stick to the facts.

If an affidavit is taken from a juvenile, the following considerations should be kept in mind. In New York State a "juvenile" is anyone from the age of 7 to the age of 16 years old. The investigator decides what type of affidavit will be taken after talking to the victim in the presence of her parents. Many juveniles in the 11 to 15 year age group make narrative affidavits. A question-and-answer affidavit is taken from a juvenile who, in the opinion of the investigator, cannot give a good affidavit in narrative form. If a question-and-answer affidavit is taken, a standard form must be followed. This is a two-officer task and all questioning of juvenile victims is done in the Youth Division. Parents are always advised what direction the officer is taking.

In most states, a juvenile under age seven should not make a statement because it is not acceptable in court. An affidavit is taken from the parent, usually the mother, who relates facts told to her by the victim. In rape cases where the victim is 11 or younger, corroboration is still required to prosecute. Without corroboration, there is no case. This makes it very important for the investigator to get in touch with all possible witnesses. He or she should try to obtain as much information from them as possible. Hopefully, they too will make statements.

In the several states which have recently dropped the corroboration requirement for all rape cases, except those with a victim younger than 11, law enforcement officials breathed a sigh of relief. However, rape is still the most difficult of all crimes to prove in court. Any additional information strengthens a case, and every detail at the scene of the crime may be pertinent. The investigator should try to obtain affidavits from all persons who had contact with the victim immediately after the rape. Affidavits from them may reveal information that the victim was unable to provide because she was too upset. Once the victim has made her statement, she will be photographed for injuries sustained during the attack. Obtaining a composite picture of the suspect is the next routine in the investigation. Often, this is an extremely upsetting experience for the victim, but the expertise of the police personnel can alleviate her distress.

THE PREVENTION OF RAPE

How many rapes could have been prevented? Those of us who work with the victims of rape look back on too many cases that never would have occurred had the woman heeded the advice of a police speaker or followed the tips in magazine and newspaper articles. Since we know that most rapes are planned, one of the most effective ways to prevent rape is to prevent the rapist from laying his plans. For example, rapists often watch potential victims through open windows. By following his victim's daily routine, the rapist learns when a woman will be alone. Open windows also provide the would-be rapist with easy access into a woman's home. Even though it may be hot in an apartment with the windows closed, it is much safer. Drawn blinds and drapes also prevent the rapist from observing his victim.

Recently, we discovered that a young mother was watched through open drapes for over a week by her attacker. Her attacker learned that her husband was away at night and picked this as the time for his attack. He drew her attention to the outside of the house and when she ran into the backyard to see what the commotion was, he raped her. Had this woman's drapes been drawn, the rapist would never have learned that the woman was alone at night.

Another obvious way to prevent a rape is to never open the door without first finding out who is there. Many women do not ask, either because they are careless or too trusting. In another recent rape, a young woman had just sent her husband off to work and her kids to school when she heard a knock on the back door. Thinking that it was a neighbor coming over to enjoy a morning cup of coffee, she opened the door without first checking who was there. She faced a youth who raped her. This victim never had a chance once her door was open. It would have been so easy for her to have asked first. Also remember that adequate locks on doors and windows prevent easy entry.

In recent years, cars have become a location for many rapes. We warn women that their own vehicle can be used against them. As precautions, women should park only in well-lighted areas, and should check for strangers following them as they approach their cars. Before entering their cars, women should check the rear seat and floor. Rapists often hide there waiting for their victims. If a woman has car trouble on the road, she should remain in her car with the doors locked and signal for help by tying a scarf or rag to her antenna. She should never accept an offer of help from anyone other than a uniformed policeman. A woman should never hitchhike or pick up hitchhikers. Women should try not to walk on the street alone. A woman alone is a potential victim, but there is safety in numbers.

Protection

One of the questions most frequently asked by women is whether they should try to defend themselves against a rapist. Advice in this area varies and depends on the circumstances of the attack. However, there is one circumstance on which all authorities agree: a woman should never attempt to fight against a weapon. It can mean her life. However, we do know of many attempted rapes in which women have lashed out against their attackers and by this quick, positive action, foiled a rape attempt. A rapist expects a passive victim and when a woman surprises him by kicking, scratching and slugging, he may be so surprised that he does not pursue his victim.

Police personnel can tell women that they carry many items in their purses that may help to thwart a rapist. Nailfiles, hairspray, hatpins, keys and rattail combs make good impromptu weapons. If a woman has the chance to use any of these, she should aim for her attacker's face. A blow on the nose or in the eyes can do a lot of damage and stun an attacker to give the woman a chance to escape. However, we must advise women that the final decision about trying to protect themselves is their responsibility. We can advise women how to protect themselves, and what the pros and cons of self-protection are; but then we must leave it up to the women to decide what they would do in the face of a rape. The best advice is, "keep your head and save your life."

7/ Suicide

Joseph T. Himmelsbach

In every state in the Union, police agencies have been charged with legal responsibilities that bring them into frequent contact with suicidal individuals. These responsibilities range from the clearly defined roles which exist when an individual threatens or attempts suicide, to situations in which an officer is called onto a scene as part of the criminal investigation of a suspicious death or accident. In addition, many suicidal situations, particularly with males, involve the use of a firearm. Such violent incidents, often resulting in public disorder of some degree, require a police response of some magnitude.

Further, there is a general expectancy in every community that police functions include aiding the suicidal person. This feeling is shared by persons at all social class levels. In every community setting, the police are traditionally viewed as the immediate help resource in emergency situations. Although most police agencies would not include the role of a suicide prevention service as one of their responsibilities, the public does utilize them in that fashion. The potential "jumper" standing precariously on a bridge is never surrounded by a squad of mental health workers attempting to lower him safely via harness and ropes.

Legal responsibility and community expectancy are the two main forces requiring police involvement with suicidal situations. Since police agencies have little choice as to whether they will or will not

respond to these forces, it is wise for police officers to become ac-
quainted with techniques and procedures for handling suicidal individuals. The material which follows will provide you with a basic
knowledge of the many different aspects of suicide. This knowledge
should help you improve your skills in dealing with suicidal people,
and, hopefully, help reduce the probability that a suicide attempt or
threat will be successful. In addition, knowledge about suicide and its
causes may tend to reduce the distress and anxiety in dealing with a
problem that usually causes discomfort for everyone involved.

We will cover three areas which relate to these goals. They are:

1. The reasons why individuals kill themselves (Theory)
2. A description of the people and methods usually involved in suicide (Demographics)
3. The actions which the police officer can take in the various suicidal situations (Intervention)

We will treat each of these areas separately; and each area will
have its own unique contribution for improving the officer's effectiveness. For example, if there were two suicidal individuals — one male
and one female — and their ages were 58 and 32 respectively, with all
other factors being relatively similar, which one would be a higher
suicidal risk? The demographics section will help you to make a more
accurate assessment of this and other situations.

THEORIES OF SUICIDAL BEHAVIOR

Man is the only animal who can make a conscious decision to
perform an act to end his own life. No other living creature possesses
that capability. When a man acts in this fashion, he is acting against
the force of all the inherited instincts which maintain his survival. A
number of theories have been developed to try to explain such human self-destruction.

Psychoanalytic Theory

One important theory for understanding suicide has come from
the theory of psychoanalysis, in particular Sigmund Freud's. He
suggested that there exist in each person two drives, the drive to live

(libido) and the drive to destruct (thanatos). The manner in which these two drives operate depends upon the fashion the person has developed for relating to his world and the people in it.

Each person, for example, has feelings that need to be satisfied (e.g., love, affection, dependency). In order to satisfy these needs, the person has to approach others in his environment. It is in establishing this relationship (between the person and the people in his environment) that the seeds for a suicidal situation may develop. For example, a conflict may occur in a relationship between two people in which affection or dependence patterns play a major role. In one of these situations, a person may be very angry or hurt at something someone has done to him. A teenage boy, for instance, may be angry with his mother for giving more attention and affection to his brothers and sisters than to him. However, he is not able to express the angry, aggressive feelings outwardly to the proper object (his mother) because he's afraid that it would end all possibility of her being close or affectionate to him again.

If this were an intense emotional situation, the individual might begin to deal with the angry feelings by focusing them inward on himself. In this situation, the individual is attempting to destroy the image of the rejecting person (mother) that he is carrying around within himself. Thus the suicidal individual's primary goal is not necessarily to take his own life, but rather to destroy the image of the person with whom he is angry, by destroying himself. This idea finds support in such explanations for a suicide attempt as "he was just trying to get back at me and make me feel guilty."

The other situation in which psychoanalytic theory finds support involves not anger over a loss, but rather a wish by the person to enter "another world" where his fantasies of "being taken care of" (dependency) will come true. Many people who are acutely suicidal believe that there is a life after death which will be less troubling for them and more rewarding. Persons who attempt suicide for this reason usually have a history of not having had their basic needs satisfied by those individuals around them. They may never have experienced the love, affection, warmth and caring which is necessary in order for every person to grow, develop and feel secure. In this system they do not look at the individuals around them as rejecting them, but rather as being indifferent to their needs. These individuals fantasize that in their "other world" people will not be indifferent to them, but rather will satisfy their needs almost without the person having to make them known. Suicide is a route for this satisfaction.

Environmental Theory

An alternate to the psychoanalytic theory of suicide has been formulated by Emile Durkheim (1951), who viewed a suicidal individual as one responding to numerous, overwhelming forces in his environment rather than to internal struggles and needs. It is Durkheim's view that individuals contemplate a suicidal act when they lack the contacts with social systems and persons in their surroundings which contribute to their sense of self. This results in a breakdown in their social integration. They then become "lost" people whose only device for resolving their dilemma is to commit suicide.

Sociologists have provided many vivid examples of suicide in response to breakdown of social integration. Periods of war, the great Depression, the recent economic difficulties in the USA all have witnessed a rise in the suicide rate. The general public is usually more understanding of this view of suicide since it involves situations which most people view as upsetting or troubling. It is reasonable to expect that as family pressures mount, and fighting and bickering increase due to financial loss, there is a higher probability of a family member thinking about suicide. Another example of the same process would be the adolescent who is the product of a broken home, who drops out of school, who is constantly being moved from relative to relative for care and who has frequent scrapes with the law. His contemplation of, or attempt at, suicide would probably come as no surprise to the counselor or probation officer working with him.

Cultural Aspects of Suicide

These are brief insights into two of many theories of suicide. In addition, the police officer should be aware of some of the cultural aspects of suicide. For example, is every person who commits suicide also mentally ill? Is the taboo against suicide universally accepted? Are there situations in which an individual should be allowed to take his life? Does a person ever have a right to take his own life? At any given time, in any given country, you may receive many different answers to these questions. There are very few absolutes in the area of suicide. The questions listed above should be considered by every person who comes into contact with a suicidal individual.

Suicide in different situations has different impacts and meanings. In Japan, suicide is a form of death which is honorable, particularly if the suicidal person has disgraced his family. In the United States, if a person who has been informed that he is terminally ill and will die a painful, prolonged death, contemplates suicide, very few people would say that he is an unreasonable or insane man. And what about the spy behind enemy lines in wartime who is caught and, rather than divulge secrets, kills himself? Finally, there is the common situation of an active, alert, older professional or businessman, for example, a judge, who is told by his doctor that he should slow down or retire because he will be dead in a year if he doesn't. The judge decides that doing nothing is a fate worse than death, so he decides to work as he has in the past and suffer the consequences. Is he suicidal? These are some of the many questions about suicide which have no certain answers. We raise them for the purpose of broadening your perspective about suicide from the view that only "crazy" people kill themselves, and it is always "wrong" or "bad" or a "shame" when they do. Suicide is much more complex than that.

WHO COMMITS SUICIDE AND HOW

Contemplating suicide, as well as actually committing the act, is not limited by race, age or socio-economic class. The methods which people use to end their lives are equally diverse, ranging from the classic jump from a bridge, to the use of a power drill to self inflict damage to the head. Within these diverse categories and methods, however, certain patterns do emerge regarding who takes their life and how. Knowing these patterns can help an officer who is planning a course of action in response to a suicide threat. We will present suicide-relevant information about five general demographic areas — age, sex, marital status, race and socio-economic class. In each area we will outline those factors which indicate high or low suicidal risk. A major portion of this information was compiled from the work of Farberow and Shneidman (1965).

Age

As a general rule, the older the individual is, the more likely he will be to successfully commit suicide. Between the ages of twenty and thirty, there are twice as many *attempts* at suicide as there are successful suicides. This ratio changes as people reach their sixties, where there are fewer attempts and more successful suicides (Farberow, 1961). There have also been some recent disturbing data which indicate that suicide by adolescents between the ages of 15 and 19 had increased by 67% in the period between 1954 and 1964. This resulted in suicide being listed as the fifth leading cause of death in that age group (Seiden, 1969).

Sex

There are striking differences between the sexes in the numbers of attempted suicides to successful suicides. Women attempt suicide much more frequently than men do; however, men have a higher rate of committing suicide than women. Various researchers have suggested different ratios, but the average ratio appears to be that for every three women who attempt suicide and fail, one woman succeeds. With men the ratio is reversed. For every man who attempts and fails there are three men who succeed. A number of theories explain these differences. In our society it is much more acceptable for women to present themselves in a weak, helpless fashion. When they are troubled it is more acceptable for them to make a "weak" suicidal gesture to cry for help than it is for men. Suicidal gesturing amongst men is often considered unmanly, weak and "chicken."

Secondly, in terms of suicidal method, men primarily employ means in which the "point of no return" is achieved more rapidly. For example, men use firearms more frequently as a method, while women ingest toxic substances (usually prescription medications). With the former situation, there is very little chance of being saved after initiating the act. Once the weapon is pointed at a vital area and the trigger pulled, the existing time for a medical rescue is short. With the latter method, depending upon the type and amount of medication, the rescue period can be anywhere from 30 minutes to 12 hours. During this time, the individual can be discovered, and medical services can be provided to neutralize the effects of the toxin.

Marital Status

In general, there are no significant differences in the successful suicide rate between those individuals who are married and those who are single (never married). However, there are significant differences between these two groups and those who are separated, widowed or divorced. In general, the rate of suicide is about four times greater in this second grouping as compared to the first.

Race

Approximately 90% of those who commit suicide are white; the remaining 10% are black or members of other minority groups. There is some indication that the minority suicide rate may be increasing. The present breakdown closely approximates the distribution ratio of white to minority population in the United States. In practical terms, an officer would be involved more frequently with suicidal individuals who are non-minority.

Some investigators have commented that the poverty level, minority suicide rate may be higher than reported due to "masked" suicides that occur. These are situations in which a suicidal person succeeds in killing himself, but not by his own hand. An example of this would be an individual who attempts an "armed" robbery in a store where almost everyone knows that the owner possesses and has used a shotgun to foil such attempts. In the course of the "robbery" the perpetrator is shot, and upon investigating, the officer finds that the person was not carrying any weapon, but behaved in such a way as to "force" the owner to fire at him. Culturally, it may be more acceptable for this individual to die in a "blaze of glory" rather than take the "coward's way out."

Socio-Economic Class

The available data suggest no significant proportional differences between various socio-economic groups, both in attempts as well as actual commits. Naturally, this would mean that there would be a greater *number* of suicides in the middle and lower middle classes, but these greater numbers are not out of proportion.

Suicide Methods

As we mentioned earlier, man is not limited in the ways he employs to "end it all." Any forensic pathologist can document the bizarre and sometimes creative means which people have used. Our review of the means of suicide in this chapter is not for the purpose of focusing on the bizarre or the sensational, but rather to provide the officer with some practical knowledge about how common and how lethal certain methods are.

As we have seen, the choice of suicide method is influenced by sex differences. Women and men tend to choose different methods. In addition, we can categorize methods in terms of levels of how lethal they are; or, more appropriately, the more abrupt versus the less abrupt method. In the former group, the person reaches the "point of no return" or the point at which medical rescue is no longer possible, more quickly than does the latter group. The most common high lethal methods are firearms, jumping from high places, cutting or piercing vital organs, and hanging. As we pointed out before, men frequently use firearms in their suicide attempts. Aside from the cultural issue mentioned earlier, men usually have easier access to firearms (e.g., hunting rifles, target pistols, etc.).

Those moderately lethal methods include drowning, poisoning (either with solids or liquids), and cutting or piercing non-vital organs. By moderately lethal, we mean the opportunity for rescue is greater. Finally, there are a group of methods which are considered low lethal. These include drowning attempts when the individual can swim, poisoning by gases, and ingesting analgesic (pain-killing) or soporific (sleep-producing) substances. Again, all of these methods can result in the death of the individual; but, they also allow the individual or another person to make efforts to neutralize their harmful effects.

Do not confuse the above scale as meaning that people who use low lethal means do not want to, or cannot kill themselves. They can. Particularly when you consider the setting in which the suicidal act is carried out. For example, an individual may decide to use a gun to end his life. If he takes a pistol and sits in the living room where his family is present, and begins to talk about "ending it all," there is a good chance that he will not attempt the act — much less, complete it. However, the same individual can check into a motel room with several vials of powerful barbiturates, put the "Do Not Disturb" sign on the door, ingest the pills with alcohol, and successfully carry out his plan.

The context and method interaction is very important for the officer to be aware of when he is responding to an attempted suicide: the presence or absence of concerned individuals when the attempt occurred; the person's relative isolation or contact with his environment; the communication of his intent to others; the location of the attempt; should all have impact on the officer's decisions for the disposition of the call.

WARNING SIGNS OF SUICIDE

It is less spectacular, but all would agree that it is better police work to prevent an armed robbery than to have to chase down the culprits. A parallel situation obviously exists with suicide. If the police officer is aware of certain warning signs of suicide intent, he may be better able to judge how severe the intent is and initiate appropriate action prior to the crisis stage. The following are some warning signs and indicators of suicide behavior that the police officer should know when he is interacting with a troubled individual, responding to a family fight, or even arresting a person who may be in a difficult situation.

Depression

A majority of individuals who contemplate suicide at some point could be considered mentally ill. The most common form of mental illness associated with suicide is depression. But depression alone is not an indicator of suicide. Probably everyone at one or several points in their lives has been depressed. However, approximately 60% of people who attempt suicide have shown some signs of being depressed prior to the act.

The signs of severe depression an officer should be aware of are of several different types. First, the individual usually appears very "sad." He or his family may report that he has been "feeling blue" or "down in the dumps" for extended periods; he may be crying, or may report that he has been crying frequently over the recent past. The individual's actions, i.e., walking, talking, etc., will appear to be slowed down; he or his family will report a loss of interest in, or motivation to do certain things, e.g., working, taking care of the household, recreation, etc. In talking with the person, his conversation may center around his inadequacies, feelings of hopelessness or of guilt.

In addition, there are some biological signs of depression which also can be present, particularly in severe cases. These signs include loss of appetite or recent weight loss; disturbance in sleep patterns, e.g., waking up at 3 or 4 a.m. and not being able to return to sleep; constipation or diarrhea; loss of interest in or pleasure from sexual activity; and easy fatigability (Beck, 1970).

Other Signs

Although signs of depression exist in a majority of suicidal cases, a significant number of suicides and suicide attempts occur without any of the overt signs mentioned above. However, there are indicators that the officer can use. These are specific to a majority of suicidal individuals, both in the depressed and the non-depressed categories. These signs center around the thoughts and actions of an individual which reflect his suicidal intent. Most suicidal persons are willing to talk about their suicidal thoughts or intent since most, if not all, persons who are suicidal continue the struggle over whether they should live or die, until their last moments. Therefore, if a police officer has a suspicion that a person is suicidal, he should not hesitate to investigate this suspicion. People often hesitate to do so for fear of "planting" ideas in a troubled person's mind. Fortunately, you can be assured that if a person has not contemplated suicide as a "solution" to his difficulties, your brief questioning in that area will not sway him to that course of action.

You can vary the sequence of the inquiry depending on the circumstances and the attitudes of the person involved. As a general rule, it is usually a good practice to begin asking questions in those areas which are not as emotionally charged, and slowly work toward the person's more troubling concerns. Farberow (1968) has suggested the following areas of investigation. As a first step, the officer should attempt to gather information about the reaction of the informant or the referring party to the suicidal person's action. If the informant appears to be concerned, caring and willing to help the person, it is a positive sign. If the informant is angry, rejecting and attempts to pass off any responsibility for the person contemplating suicide, it is a negative sign.

The officer then might ask about the presence of any severe, recent or chronic, medical problems. The presence of medical difficulties such as cancer, severe heart problems, etc., increases the risk of the person carrying out a suicidal act. Another area which has a similar contributing effect is a recent loss. The loss can be due to any one of a number of events: death of a close family member (husband or wife), loss of a job or other financial setback, or rejection by a partner through a divorce, separation or "lover's quarrel." The presence of any of these or other losses increases the risk of a successful suicide.

If an officer learns that many of these variables are present, he should not hesitate to talk to the person about the possibility that he might be considering suicide. An effective way of broaching the topic is to say, "Often when people feel the way you feel, and have gone through some of the things you've gone through lately, such as (. . . .) sometimes they think about taking their life. Have you been having any thoughts like that?" Approaching the subject in this fashion is usually much more effective than saying, "Boy, you have it rough, did you ever think about killing yourself?" This latter statement serves to make the individual defensive, while the former indicates a level of understanding which allows the two to communicate more closely.

If the person says he's not thinking about suicide, the officer should accept this, unless he has significant additional evidence to the contrary. If the person says, "Yes, I am thinking about taking my life," then it is very important to ask certain follow-up questions. These follow-up questions refer to how, if at all, the person intends to carry out the act. This information should include specifics about time, place and method, as well as the means for carrying out the plan. The officer should compare the information received with the high-low lethality criteria we mentioned before. If, for example, the person responds by saying he has vague diffuse feelings of "being better off dead" with no specific means to that end, he is not as highly suicidal as the person who can give specific information that he plans to "take his hunting rifle, drive to a secluded wooded area and pull the trigger."

One very important piece of additional information which the officer should also investigate at this time is the subject's history of previous attempts at suicide. The absence of any previous experience is a positive sign, the presence of previous efforts, particularly severe or of the high lethal variety, is a negative sign. Because individuals have attempted suicide before and failed, does not mean they were not "serious" about it then or now. A majority of successful suicides have been preceded by one or more unsuccessful tries.

These "negative" variables can be counterbalanced somewhat by the presence of certain "positive" characteristics. The first is the individual's ability to communicate with others about his feelings of despair, loneliness, etc., and to keep "in contact" with those in his environment. The danger of suicide increases when the individual withdraws from others and breaks off communication. Another positive characteristic is the presence of resources which can support the individual through the difficult and stressful time. Support and concern are available from many different sources: clergy, physicians, family members and friends. It is when these supports are absent or exhausted that the risk of suicide increases.

Other Variables

Finally, we want to mention three situations which, if present, reduce the ability of any professional, police or mental health worker, to make an accurate judgment of suicidal risk. The three variables are the presence of:

1. chronic drug abuse
2. alcoholism
3. psychosis

Each of these problems can result in unpredictable behavior on the part of the would-be suicide. Chronic drug abusers may become suicidal as they ingest increasing amounts of medications to obtain "the high," without realizing the added risks involved. Their suicide may be "unintentional" but is nonetheless fatal.

Alcoholics, as a group, at one time were felt to have the same suicide rate as the general population. Recent data (Litman and Wold, 1975), however, suggest that they have a much higher suicide rate. In addition, they are less able to control their self-destructive behavior or ask for help while they're in an alcoholic stupor. Added to this is the potent effect that alcohol has on modern drugs, with the result that alcoholics are a high lethal group. Lastly, those individuals who are classified as "psychotic" present particular problems when they are also suicidal, due to the fact that they are "out of touch with reality." This makes the officer's job even more difficult since it becomes harder to pick out the events that are causing the psychotic person's suicidal action. The officer may be more successful in dealing with this last category of persons by using the suggestions on dealing with the mentally ill outlined in Chapter 4. If the officer discovers that any of the three situations mentioned above are present, he should respond as if a warning flag were raised. Because of their very nature, they must be approached with more caution than the usual suicidal attempt.

Context of Suicidal Behavior

It is important to remember that suicide is not a solitary act that occurs in a vacuum. The suicidal person operates in a family or social system which influences or perhaps causes him to act. The alert, effective officer must remain aware of the social context of the act, as well as the individual issues as presented above.

A frequently heard phrase which supports the interpersonal aspect of suicide is, "He/she is only doing that (suicide attempt) for attention." Unfortunately, there are occasions in which people agree that that statement is correct, and so they may ignore the suicidal act or even subject the suicidal person to ridicule. Many suicide attempts occur because the individuals feel powerless or incapable of effecting a change in those around them. The suicide can be an attempt to force a change in an intolerable or overwhelming situation. For example, a wife who feels that her marriage is undesirable because of her husband's insensitivity to her needs may attempt suicide as a way of overcoming the "barriers" which stand between them.

Another interpersonal issue which can contribute to suicidal action is the wish on the part of an individual to cause another person to feel guilty due to a real or imagined wrong done to them. Their goal may be to make the other person feel "bad" because they were hurt by them. This process occurs many times in the rejected lover syndrome where the rejected party wants to "get back at" the person who hurt him. This can become a volatile situation since the suicidal person's goal may be to have that individual carry around the guilt over the death for the rest of his or her life. If that level of hurt or anger is present, then the suicidal person may be unresponsive to attempts at "reconciliation."

Finally, there is the interpersonal situation in which an individual contemplates and acts on his suicidal thoughts as a way of preventing himself from being punished for a real or imagined wrong he has committed. The fear of being "found out" — for example, a respected businessman being arrested on a morals charge — can cause many persons to attempt suicide. Included in this category are those individuals who feel that they have failed their families or loved ones when they have not been successful in school or in business.

How the suicidal person's social system responds to his or her attempt is an important factor in judging whether the act may occur again. If the people who are the objects of the action do not respond in the manner or degree the person attempting suicide desires, the probability exists that the person will make repeated attempts with increased lethality.

OFFICER'S ACTIONS IN SUICIDAL SITUATIONS

Any action dealing with persons in stress must have its roots in understanding what that person may be experiencing. If such understanding is absent, the actions which are taken may often be chaotic, disorganized and often dangerous. Knowing certain minimal information about the person and his context remarkably improves the officer's effectiveness on the scene. With this understanding as a foundation, the officer should be familiar with certain techniques and procedures which can be effective in dealing with the suicidal person. Toward this goal, we will divide this section into three general areas:

1. Actions to be taken prior to the actual suicide attempt.
2. Actions to be taken after the attempt has occurred or while it is occurring.
3. Actions to be taken if the attempt is successful.

In each of these areas, certain "Do's" and "Don'ts" will be outlined.

Actions Prior to the Suicidal Action

Police officers can be called to a pre-suicidal scene at any point from the time the person just talks about taking his or her life to the time the person is about to pull the trigger. Families call the police when they fear that a family member is "about to do something drastic." Citizens contact police when a suicidal person goes public in his attempt, e.g., the bridge jumper. The officer can use the following procedures in a variety of situations to prevent the act from being carried out.

Safety issues. In any crisis situation, one might have the tendency to rush headlong into the scene in order to make an immediate rescue. Every effort should be made by the officer to control this tendency. All too often, unwise and unplanned action can result in injury or death to the subject as well as to on-lookers and officers themselves. Keep in mind that if the attempt is that imminent, there is very little you can do to prevent it. If the person is using a firearm or jumping in his attempt, you have no way of blocking that action quickly. Therefore, your first step should be to assess any threats to your safety or the safety of others in the environment. This is particularly important when the suicidal person is holding a firearm.

Secondly, the officer should attempt to secure the scene as well as he can. This includes moving disruptive or out-of-control family members to another part of the house, or outside if necessary; insuring that the physical environment is as safe as possible under the circumstances; and positioning himself so he can see all the people involved, i.e., his partner, family members and subject.

Finally, the officer should try to gain as much accurate information as possible from a reliable source (e.g., a person's spouse) concerning events immediately preceding the officer's being called, recent stresses or unusual occurrences in the family, the subject's history of suicide attempts, the subject's access to weapons or pills, the layout of a room if the subject has blocked access to it, the subject's present mood (e.g., agitated, depressed, withdrawn, angry, etc.), as well as the name or names of people the subject may trust. These actions can be carried out in a brief period of time (five to ten minutes). When completed, the officer will be in a better position to initiate his contact with the subject.

Initial contact. From the outset, it is very important that the officer project a certain attitude to the person he is helping. This attitude can be best described as one of concern, caring and absence of threat. There is little to be gained by comments such as, "You're just looking for attention," or "Stop this nonsense and grow up!" They place the person on the defensive.

The officer's first verbal contact should be to introduce himself by name and tell the subject why he's on the scene. Often it's helpful to give your full name such as, "I'm Officer Bill Smith." This allows the person to respond to the officer on a more personal and informal basis if he chooses to use his first name. In giving the reasons why he is on the scene, the officer should be honest and straightforward. For example, "We were called by your family because they were afraid that you may want to hurt yourself, and we're here to see if we can help you." Essentially, this is the main reason why police are called. The stated goal is not to lock somebody up but rather to help the troubled individual.

The next step is to determine what the person prefers to be called. Most people will not say, "Call me Mr. Jones," but, rather, will give their first names or common nicknames. This again allows for a more personal communication relationship to develop, which should be the officer's goal. Following this initial interaction, the officer, knowing certain information from the first related contact, can begin talking about the problem areas. It is very important that the officer convey to the subject at this point that the subject has the upper hand. A suicidal person is taking the ultimate action for controlling his own fate. If he feels that the police or others are going to wrest this control from him, he will play out the scene rather quickly with tragic consequences.

The officer, through the use of words and gestures, can communicate to the troubled person that he is not about to threaten or take over his control. However, an interesting process now occurs. The officer, in a sense, is giving permission to the person that he be in charge. However, the only people who can give "permission" to another to be in charge are other individuals of higher authority. So by saying to the subject, "You're calling the shots, we'll listen to you," the officer is subtly, but effectively, beginning to move toward controlling the situation. This attitude can be conveyed in other ways; for example, asking the person's permission to sit in a chair or enter the room, etc. All of these actions serve to reduce threat and thus assist the subject in becoming more relaxed and open to verbal intervention.

Once the officer has been able to communicate this non-threatening stance, he will usually receive a positive response to a question such as, "What do you think is going on, how do you see this situation?" The officer should expect a brief reply to this question such as, "Things just haven't been going right." At this point, the officer is beginning to gain control of the situation. He can ask the individual to explain about the "things" or what isn't "right," etc. The officer is accomplishing three things at the same time:

1. He is gaining more information about the person's problems, lethality, etc.
2. He is developing some insight into the way this particular person thinks.
3. He is allowing the person to vent some of his pent-up feelings to an unbiased listener (i.e., not a family member or friend). The process of venting feelings serves to reduce the tension that the person is experiencing, and as a consequence may reduce the drive to commit suicide.

As the subject is talking about his difficulties and his situation, the officer should be alert and responsive. The subject's talking should not be seen as a "time waster" to allow for more reinforcements to arrive, etc. It is a basic part of handling a suicidal person. The officer should be gently probing with questions so that he can gain as much factual data as possible in order to rate the person's lethality using the criteria we mentioned before.

Do's and Don'ts. While dealing with the subject, the officer should be following certain Do's and Don'ts.

1. Do listen. Be attentive to what the person is saying, ask clarifying questions, ask the person to continue, indicate by facial and body cues that you are attending to him.
2. Do give honest responses. That is, do not lie to the individual about the consequences of his actions or your feelings about what he is doing. However, be careful about being cast into the role of "judge and jury." For example, the person may ask if you "feel it's terrible when a man can't support his family properly?" If

you say yes, then you may have supported one of the causes of the suicide.

3. Do attempt to understand the person's view. This does not mean you *agree* with his view but rather you *understand* how he is viewing the events which have happened to him. This understanding gives him an ally.

4. Don't give advice. As the saying goes, "Advice is cheap." The suicidal person has probably been "talked at" for many months. People love to help others by telling them what to do and why. However, this is rarely helpful to the emotionally troubled person. They usually know what they should do, but, emotionally, they are blocked from doing it. Telling them what to do may increase their feelings of failure and inadequacy and heighten their suicidal intent.

5. Don't belittle their actions. Occasionally, when individuals attempt to assist a suicidal person, they make misguided attempts to "shock" the person back to reality. They do so by "calling their bluff" or by minimizing their attempt. For example, a response to a person's unsuccessful wrist cutting could be "You really botched it, next time you should cut deeper." Unfortunately, the person may act on this misguided advice. In addition, one should be careful about minimizing the person's problems. What may appear to be insignificant to you may be overwhelming to them. If you indicate that you feel his are minor issues, you lose your opportunity to understand what really is occurring in the situation.

6. Don't be judgmental. Most people contemplating suicide are victims of very harsh internal judges, and this judge may have already passed sentence. A suicidal person will not respond positively to having another judge enter the scene.

7. Do create rapport with the individual. The officer should indicate legitimate agreements between himself and the subject in as many areas (particularly non-emotional ones) as possible. Some examples of this might be their agreeing on how difficult it is to raise and care for a family, the problems of lack of enough money, current social issues, personal likes and dislikes in such areas as sports, food, entertainment, etc. Again, this serves to ally the officer with the subject, helps develop the relationship between them,

and allows the subject to feel that the officer can understand him since they have some similar background.

If the police officer who intervenes follows these brief suggestions, he or she will improve the chances of preventing a suicidal act from being carried out. At this point in the intervention, the officer has developed an adequate information base, made an initial contact, projected an attitude of concern, and followed certain accepted ways of interacting with a troubled individual.

Content themes. For the types of intervention we suggest here, it is not necessary for the officer to respond to every issue the subject raises. Instead of responding to particular issues, he should try to be alert to particular themes that are present in the subject's story. In a majority of situations, one or two themes will be present: either a feeling of hopelessness and helplessness, or a feeling of anger and disgust. This latter feeling may be prompted by wanting to "get back at" someone the subject feels may have hurt him.

Once the general theme becomes apparent, the officer can respond to the theme in an appropriate fashion. In the situation where the person is feeling hopeless or helpless, the officer's response should be one of providing hope. As we indicated earlier, all suicidal individuals have a part of themselves that wants to live. The hope-providing message can be directed to that part that is seeking life. The officer can provide hope by indicating that other people he has dealt with in similar situations have handled their problems with proper help. He can also indicate that there are specially trained people (psychologists, social workers, etc.) who are concerned about people, as he is, who also can help. These are two of many "hope/help-providing" comments that can be effective.

If the situation appears to be one which reflects mostly anger and disgust, the officer's response should be different. In these situations, the suicide may be an attempt to get back at or hurt another individual. The person contemplating suicide may be justified in his or her rage toward these other persons. The response which the officer would seek to relate to this person is twofold: a) recognizing the subject's anger and disgust so as to legitimize it; and, b) offering the possibility of more effective alternatives than suicide for dealing with such feelings. The most valid point the officer can make in this regard is that suicide is a very costly and ineffective means to that end. Other methods can be used to deal with all types of interpersonal problems without the supreme consequence of ending your life.

Suicide is often discussed as a solution to difficulties. Most suicidal people will indicate that they have tried all other options. However, the officer will probably discover, by questioning the person, that only a few solutions have been thought of, much less attempted. Just the opportunity to discuss the problems or difficulties with an individual who is trained and who is objective will often produce new, more realistic solutions.

Referral. When a situation lends itself to the interventions described above, the natural closing point should be a referral to a mental health agency. The officer should realize that the most effective referral in each situation may vary from an inpatient psychiatric admission to an outpatient visit. This referral should be made in consultation with a person from a mental health agency; and the officer's involvement should end once this is accomplished.

Use of Force in Responding to Suicidal Attempts

The description of an intervention with suicidal individuals and the various techniques you can use is obviously an ideal portrayal. It would be a rare event if all components were present. But, it is safe to say that you'll find a majority of the issues described in many different suicide attempts.

Occasionally an officer may be caught with an unexpected happening even though he may have been responding in a most appropriate and competent fashion. This can occur, for example, if another family member unexpectedly disrupts the rapport the officer has established, or the officer unwittingly opens an area of discussion which is highly emotionally charged. At this point, in the officer's presence, the person may attempt to carry out the suicidal attempt. Unfortunately, if this begins to occur, the officer has no other choice than to respond as quickly as possible to interrupt the act (e.g., to disarm the person, grab the pills, or tackle the would-be jumper). Such actions can and do create much confusion and run the risk of injuring not only the subject but also the officers involved. It is a necessary risk. Once the attempt is interrupted in this fashion, the individual has usually passed the "peak moment" and will probably not continue to make subsequent attempts at that time.

Responding after an Unsuccessful or Non-Fatal Attempt

Police are also called upon to respond after an unsuccessful suicide attempt has occurred. Your first responsibility in such circumstances is to insure that the individual's needs are met. The officer should provide first aid and call for medical assistance if necessary. In terms of his personal response to the subject, he will usually find that the subject is more cooperative, less agitated, and, at times, almost serene. It is as if he accomplished his goal in the attempt, and at this point the struggle is over. The officer should focus on his concern for the individual, his willingness to help him and make him comfortable. The subject may respond by requesting that he be allowed to die. The officer should respond by pointing out that it's his job to protect people, and he cannot allow someone to kill himself.

In addition to responding to the medical and psychological needs of the victim, the officer should give the family information about what they can expect and what will happen to their relative. Such information could include where the person is to be treated medically, and the location of the psychiatric facility the person will probably be admitted to.

Officer's Response to a Successful Suicide

In a situation where the person's suicidal action was fatal, it is the officer's responsibility to perform the legal duty of investigating a suspicious death. Very little is written about this aspect of suicide. However, it is a situation which every police officer in the course of his or her career will face repeatedly. Shneidman (1970) has summarized the type of information which the officer should obtain. The first element is the description of the death. Included in this is a description of the appearance and location of the body. The method of death should be reconstructed by examining the surroundings. Firearms, pills, etc., which may be suspected as methods should be booked as evidence. The officer should also try to determine how the method was obtained.

The second element is the interview with those persons who have discovered the body, and with an individual who was on initimate terms with the subject. The officer should ask particularly about the subject's actions during his last hours of life. Finally, the officer should pay particular attention to finding out, from a knowledgeable informant, the habits of the deceased, especially with regard to the method used for death. For example, did the subject know about or use firearms? Did the subject have access to drugs and if so, how did he use them? Was there any evidence of mental disturbance? Any recent changes in the subject's life style or personality? Any recent stresses or illnesses or arrests?

Information gathered in this fashion will be very helpful for determining whether a given death is a suicide. Often, physical evidence such as a suicide note is necessary to help establish whether the cause of death was a suicide. There may be times when this becomes particularly difficult because family members for various reasons attempt to confuse a situation by altering evidence which points to suicide, such as destroying suicide notes. This is in part due to the continued existence of moral stigma and insurance difficulties attached to suicide.

Along with the need to define a member's death as "not a suicide," family survivors, particularly those with a close relationship to the deceased, may experience a number of reactions and feelings. Farberow (1968) has outlined several of them, and the officer should be prepared to expect these to occur when interviewing family members. They may include:

1. Strong feelings of loss, accompanied by sorrow and mourning.
2. Strong feelings of anger for:
    a) being made to feel responsibility, or
    b) being rejected (e.g., what was offered was refused).
3. Guilt, shame or embarrassment with feelings of responsibility for the death.
4. Feelings of failure or inadequacy that what was needed could not be supplied.
5. Feelings of relief that the nagging, consistent demands have ceased.
6. Feelings of having been deserted, especially true for children.
7. Ambivalence with a mixture of all of the above.
8. Reactions of doubt and self-questioning whether enough was attempted.

9. Denial that a suicide has occurred, with a possibility of a conspiracy of silence among all concerned.
10. Arousal of one's own impulses toward suicide.

It is not necessary for the officer to respond to all of these feelings, but he should be aware of their existence and be sensitive to them. This will allow him to complete his responsibilities more quickly, and avoid any unnecessary confrontations with family members whom he may view as obstructing his investigation.

* * *

Suicide and suicide attempts are always tragic and unsettling situations. Confronting and dealing with the individuals and families involved is uncomfortable, even for the most experienced mental health professional. However, the payoff of knowing that you have helped a person back to life is likewise very rewarding. In this chapter we have attempted to provide certain fundamental information so that police officers may experience that reward.

References

Beck, A.T. Depression: Causes and treatment. Philadelphia: University of Pennsylvania Press, 1970.

Conklin, G. Personal communication, Syracuse, 1975.

Durkheim, E. *Suicide: A study in sociology.* New York: Free Press, 1951.

Farberow, N.L., & Shneidman, E.S. (Eds.). *The cry for help.* New York: McGraw-Hill, 1961.

Farberow, N.L. Suicide: Psychological aspects. In D. Sills (Ed.), *The international encyclopedia of the social sciences.* New York: Crowell, Collier & Macmillan, 1968.

Litman, R.E., & Wold, C.I. *Controlled study of an anti-suicide program.* Paper presented at Annual Meeting of American Psychiatric Association, May 1975.

Seiden, R.A. *Suicide among youth* (Supplement to the Bulletin of Suicidology). Washington, D.C.: U.S. Government Printing Office, 1969.

Shneidman, E.S., Farberow, N.L., & Litman, R.E. *The psychology of suicide.* New York: Science House, 1970.

III

Training Police in Crisis Intervention Skills

A Method for Effective Training: Structured Learning

Structured Learning Manual for Police Trainers

8/ A Method for Effective Training: Structured Learning

We have written Chapters 8 and 9 for the police *trainer;* that is, the person involved in teaching police officer trainees the crisis intervention skills and materials presented in the preceding chapters. In Chapter 2 we examined, in considerable detail, what skills the effective officer should possess in crisis situations; and, in Chapters 3 through 7 provided detailed information regarding specific types of crises — information which hopefully can add further to the officer's crisis intervention effectiveness. But, before we can maximize officer effectiveness, we must concern ourselves not only with *what* the officer must know, but also with *how* he can best learn it.

An officer could, for example, simply *read* about crisis intervention procedures (Chapter 2); and read the information in the chapters dealing with types of crises. Much of what we all learn comes from "instructional" reading. Thus, trying to learn crisis intervention procedures by reading about them would certainly succeed to some extent. Or, instead of asking you to read these materials, we could ask you to listen to a series of *lectures* dealing with the same crisis intervention content. As is true with reading as a learning method, we would also expect lectures to result in some gains in knowledge.

But, reading and listening to lectures are both passive learning techniques. In both instances the officer takes no action, tries out none of the procedures, practices nothing. For this reason, passive learning approaches often fail to bring about either enduring learning or transfer effects. That is, the officer will tend to forget what he has (passively) learned. Or, even if he does remember much of it, he often will not know how to use or apply this knowledge where it counts — on patrol. Thus, a crucial characteristic of the training approach we will recommend in this chapter is that it requires active learning — learning by doing — by the officer-trainee.

But, learning by doing is not the only necessary requirement of effective training approaches. After all, much current police training which occurs by "learning on the road" is learning by doing. Such learning via the successes and failures of daily patrol experiences is, however, very inefficient and often dangerous. Certainly, we all learn from experience; but, it is both a waste of time and effort, and unnecessarily risky, to learn most of what we should know about handling crisis calls only by going on such calls. The rookie learning this way may have a poor teacher, or worse, he may make an error which results in serious injury, or his death.

Just as the airplane pilot learns by "doing" in a cockpit simulator — in which wasted time is greatly reduced, and real risks to himself and others are essentially eliminated — we would recommend a training approach which also uses simulation. It is, to be sure, less "real" than learning on patrol. But, learning crisis intervention procedures by having trainees respond to simulated crises in a classroom has been shown to be a rapid and safe way to teach skills which do endure and do transfer to real-life settings. Thus, the training method we will propose requires active learning by trainees, and involves use of simulation in the form of guided and gradual use of classroom practice and role playing activities.

There is one further general quality which an effective training method should possess. It should aim at teaching the officer trainee new behaviors, and not, primarily, new attitudes. Procedures which seek mostly to change trainee attitudes, such as T-groups, sensitivity groups, Transactional Analysis and the like, very often fail to result in changed trainee behavior. Officers may feel differently about what they are doing, but they do much the same thing as they've done before!

Our definition of the officer who is effective in response to crisis calls is one who has learned a variety of behaviors which produce the desired effects on the citizens or disputants involved. The effective officer has not only learned this range of calming, information-gathering and crisis-resolving behaviors, but he is flexible enough and skilled enough to be willing and able to use the right behaviors with the right citizen at the right time. With these general qualities of effective training in mind, let us now turn to the specific procedures we wish to recommend to those involved in training police officers for effective crisis intervention.

STRUCTURED LEARNING TRAINING

Structured Learning Training (SLT) consists of four procedures, each of which has been shown to have a substantial and reliable effect on learning. These procedures are modeling, role playing, social reinforcement or other corrective feedback, and transfer training. In each training session, typically involving two trainers and eight to twelve trainees, the trainees are:

1. Played a brief videotape (or shown live "models") depicting the specific skill behaviors or learning points that make up effective police action (modeling).
2. Given substantial opportunity and encouragement to behaviorally rehearse or practice the effective behaviors shown to them by the models (role playing).
3. Provided with corrective feedback, especially in the form of approval or praise, as their role playing of the learning point behaviors becomes more and more similar to the tape or live model's behavior (social reinforcement).
4. Asked to participate in all of these procedures in such a way that transfer of the newly learned behaviors from the training setting to real-life patrol settings will be highly likely (transfer training).

The specifics of how to use this combination of training procedures in the best manner, to teach crisis intervention skills, are presented in step-by-step detail in the next chapter. To aid you in understanding and using these procedures most effectively, we will describe their background and development, as well as other successful uses to which each has been put.

Modeling

Modeling, often also called "imitation" or "observational learning," has been shown time and again to be an effective, reliable and rapid technique both for learning new behaviors or skills, and for strengthening or weakening previously learned behaviors or skills. The variety and sheer number of different behaviors learned, strengthened, or weakened due to seeing a model engage in the behavior is quite impressive. Yet, it must be noted that each day most individuals observe dozens and perhaps hundreds of behaviors by others which they do not imitate.

In addition to such live models, we read a newspaper and watch television perhaps every day, and see very polished models of purchasing behavior, but do not run out to the store and buy the product. And, as police or others involved in dealing with citizens in crisis, we are often exposed to expensively produced, expertly acted, and seemingly persuasive instructional films, but we remain uninstructed. In short, though we are surrounded by all sorts of models engaged in a wide variety of behaviors, we only imitate a very few, and we do so very selectively. To maximize trainee learning, the trainer making use of modeling procedures, as in SLT, is well-advised to be familiar with those characteristics of the model himself, of the way the modeling behavior is shown, and of the trainee, all of which make learning from modeling more likely to occur.

Model characteristics. Greater modeling will occur when the person to be imitated (the model), as compared to the trainee, is:

1. Highly competent or expert
2. Of high rank or status
3. Of the same sex
4. Controls resources desired by the trainee
5. Friendly and helpful
6. Rewarded for engaging in the particular behaviors

Modeling display characteristics. Greater modeling will occur when the taped, filmed or live modeling display shows the model(s) performing the behaviors we want the trainee to imitate:

1. In a vivid and detailed manner
2. In order from least to most difficult

3. With considerable repetition
4. With a minimum of irrelevant details (behaviors *not* to be imitated)
5. By use of at least a few different models

Trainee characteristics. Greater learning by imitation will occur when the trainee:

1. Is instructed to imitate
2. Is similar to the model in background or attitudes
3. Likes the model
4. Is rewarded for engaging in the particular behaviors

Research on the effectiveness of learning by modeling has been so positive that you may wonder about the necessity for the other components of SLT. If so many different behaviors have been altered successfully by having trainees watch and listen to a model displaying the behaviors, why are role playing, social reinforcement and transfer training necessary?

The answer is clear. Modeling alone is insufficient because, though it yields many positive learning effects, they are very often not enduring effects. The police recruit may watch an experienced officer issue a traffic citation to a citizen, and, at that point in time, know how to do so himself. But, if he doesn't participate more actively in the learning process, the trainee is not likely to know how to perform this action effectively for very long. Active participation aids enduring learning.

Structured Learning Training seeks its effectiveness from elements which even go beyond the proven value of active participation. Modeling teaches the trainee *what* to do. To perform what he has observed in an effective and enduring manner, he also needs sufficient practice to know *how* to do it, and sufficient reward to motivate him, or, in effect, tell him *why* he should do it. Modeling shows the *what*, role playing teaches the *how*, social reinforcement provides the *why*. Each alone is not enough; together they offer most of what is necessary for effective and enduring learning. Let us, therefore, turn to the second component of SLT, role playing.

Role Playing

If trainees are to learn how to do something, they must try it. To try many behaviors relevant to effective police functioning under safe conditions, there must be a somewhat "pretend" quality to the try out. As role playing is used in SLT, this pretend quality is minimized, while a quality of realism is maximized. Officer-trainees do not act out a script prepared for them in advance; but, following the exact learning point outline illustrated in the modeling display, act out the learning point behaviors as they think would be most effective for them, in their patrol area, with particular citizens from this area.

Thus, in SLT, role playing is not just acting, or psychodrama, or general simulation. It is, instead, behavioral rehearsal — made real for the trainee in every respect possible. This "rehearsal for reality" quality of the use of role playing in SLT, as you will see later in this chapter, increases the chances that what the trainee learns in the training setting will be used in the application setting, i.e., on patrol.

A considerable amount of research has been conducted on the effectiveness of role playing as a training technique. In much of this research, a group of people who share certain attitudes are identified, and then divided into three subgroups. One group, role players, are then asked to give speeches which take a position *opposite* to their real attitudes. The second group, listen only, hear these speeches but make no speeches of their own. The third group, control, neither give nor hear these speeches. Results of these studies show that role players change their attitudes away from their original ones and toward that of the speeches they made, significantly more than either the listen only or control groups. Role playing has been shown to effectively contribute to attitude change (as well as behavior change) in a wide variety of educational, industrial, clinical and other settings.

As was true for the modeling component of SLT, there are steps you may take to increase the likelihood that role playing will lead to effective learning. Details concerning these "role-play enhancers" are presented in the next chapter; but, in overview here, role playing is more likely to result in trainee learning when the trainee:

1. Feels he has some choice about whether or not to participate in the role playing.
2. Is committed to what he role plays in the sense that he role plays publicly, openly, and in front of others who know him.
3. Improvises in role playing, rather than following a set script.
4. Is rewarded or reinforced for his role playing performance.

We pointed out earlier that modeling was a necessary part of effective training, but that modeling alone was not sufficient for enduring learning. Role playing may similarly be viewed as a necessary but insufficient training procedure. After seeing effective police action correctly illustrated (modeling), and trying it himself (role playing), the trainee still needs an answer regarding *why* he should consistently use the given approach on patrol. What is his motivation, his incentive, his reward? The trainer's answer to this, we would suggest, is social reinforcement.

Social Reinforcement

Psychologists interested in improving the effectiveness of teaching have drawn an important distinction between acquiring knowledge and actually using it; or, to state it in their words, between *learning* and *performance*. Learning is knowing what to do and how to do it. Performance is actually doing what we have learned. As we said earlier in this chapter, modeling teaches what to do; role playing teaches how to do it. Thus, both modeling and role playing affect learning, not performance. Competent performance (in this case, whether the trainee will actually perform what he has learned in the training center) occurs because of other events — especially the reward or reinforcement the trainee receives for his role playing.

In SLT, both the trainers and the other trainees in the group have the responsibility of giving corrective feedback to the trainee who has role played. Most of this feedback involves telling the trainee how well his role-play enactment of the skill's learning points matched the same learning points as portrayed by the model on the modeling display. As the trainee's role playing becomes more and more similar to the model's enactment, the feedback increasingly takes the form of approval, praise, compliments and similar social reinforcement. It is this type of feedback which provides the motivation and incentive to continue performing well what the role player has learned.

Just as there are "rules" which, if applied, improve the effectiveness of modeling and role playing, there are a number of research findings which help us improve the effect of social reinforcement on performance. The effect of reinforcement on performance is increased when:

1. There is minimal delay between the completion of the behavior

to be reinforced and the delivery of the reinforcement or reward.
2. It is made clear to the trainee which specific behaviors are being reinforced.
3. The nature of the reinforcement being offered is actually perceived as a reward by the trainee.
4. The amount of reinforcement being offered is actually perceived as a reward by the trainee.
5. After making sure the trainee is performing well, the trainer reinforces only some, but not all, performances of the behavior.

At this point in the training sequence, the trainee has learned what to do, practiced how to do it, and been given incentive to perform it well at the training center. What is missing, and what absolutely must be provided, are procedures to increase the chances he will also perform the newly learned skills where they count most, in his real-life setting — on patrol.

Transfer Training

Transfer training is a crucial part of any training program. In the training center, away from the pressures of daily patrol, and with the helpful support and encouragement of both the trainers and other trainees, most trainees can learn well and perform competently. It is unfortunate that so many training programs accept competent performance *in the training center* as the criterion for evaluating the success or failure of the program.

While successful trainee performance in the training center is an obvious prerequisite to successful application on patrol, it is very far from a guarantee of it. In fact, more programs fail to transfer than succeed! To maximize the chances that the trainee will be able to transfer his training gains, you are encouraged to reflect the following transfer training principles in your training procedures:

1. General principles. Transfer of training is increased by providing the trainee with the general principles, reasons or rules which underlie the procedures and techniques being taught. If the police officer trainee understands *why* certain of his behaviors are likely to lead to certain citizen reactions, he is more likely to know how and when to apply these behaviors on patrol.

2. Response availability. The more we have practiced something in the past, the more likely we will be able to perform it correctly when necessary. In many training programs, the trainee is required to demonstrate that he can perform a given skill, and once he does so once, the trainer moves on to teaching the next skill. Research on "overlearning" clearly shows that this training strategy is an error. Transfer is increased if trainees are required to perform the correct behaviors not once or twice, but many times. Such repetition may seem unnecessary to some trainees, and they may even complain of boredom; but the correct responses will be more available if overlearning has occurred. Thus, you should encourage trainees to repeat correct skill behaviors many times as a training technique.

3. Identical elements. The greater the similarity between the training setting and the application setting, the greater the transfer. We may all prefer to go on "retreat" to a comfortable training center when training is to occur, but the more realistic the setting, the better. This may mean that the ideal training context for police officers should contain many of the same physical and interpersonal characteristics as being on patrol. Patrol itself may be "too real" for much of the initial training of officers, but a simulation set-up which is as lifelike as possible should be attempted. The behavior of partners, citizens, disputants and others in the training setting should resemble their real-life counterparts as much as possible — as should the physical mock-up of patrol cars and crisis scenes.

As training progresses, and once the officer possesses a foundation of basic, useful skills, these skills will ideally shift out of the center into actual patrol cars on patrol. Thus, there most certainly is a place for "learning on the road," but it must be preceded by learning from a trainer in a training center.

4. Performance feedback. The evaluations and reactions of other people to things we do determines to a great extent whether or not we keep doing them. A trainee may have learned a skill very well in a training center; been socially reinforced by the trainers there; and provided with the transfer-enhancers of general principles, overlearning and identical elements; but, the skills may still fail to transfer to the real world of everyday patrol. This can and does occur when the real-life evaluators of our behavior are either indifferent or critical.

Command personnel, the road-wise and experienced partner, and similar highly credible rewarders can make or break a training program. If such respected sources recognize trainee skill behavior with approval, praise or other social reinforcement, the skill behavior will continue to transfer. If the behavior is, instead, either ignored or criticized, it will tend to disappear rapidly. So, our training program can get new skill behaviors started, the other three transfer-enhancers can help keep it going, but the feedback trainees get will be especially critical for its continuance.

Research in support of this position is so clear that we urge trainers to maximize positive performance feedback by meeting with command and related personnel, and actually training them in what trainee behaviors to look for and encourage, and in procedures for rewarding the trainee when the behavior is skilled and competent. If command support does not exist, if they are indifferent or opposed to the training effort and this attitude proves to be unchangeable, we firmly recommend that you do not undertake the training effort.

APPLICATIONS OF STRUCTURED LEARNING TRAINING

In this chapter, we have begun to introduce the reader to the four procedures which constitute SLT, and certain means for increasing their effectiveness. This combination of training techniques has been used successfully to teach a wide variety of skills to numerous types of trainees: management skills to those in industry; social skills to shy and reserved persons; disciplining skills to teachers; empathy skills to parents; helper skills to nurses; self-management skills to patients; negotiation skills to disputants; and, as we will describe in the chapter which follows, crisis intervention skills to police officers. In this next chapter we will provide the specific and detailed guidelines and materials for you, the trainer, to use to teach crisis intervention skills to police officers.

9/ Structured Learning Manual for Police Trainers

The primary purpose of this chapter is to provide detailed guidelines for effectively conducting structured learning training of police officers in crisis intervention skills. Structured learning is a training approach which has been successful in teaching police officers, supervisors and a variety of other trainees, the skills helpful to them in leading satisfying and effective lives at work and elsewhere.

The police officer is confronted almost every day, with highly emotional citizens. On fight, accident, assault, rape and suicide calls, and when dealing with upset, fearful, confused or angry people, he must be skilled in dealing effectively and rapidly with charged emotions. He must, often in rapid sequence, protect his own safety, calm the situation, gather relevant information, and take appropriate action. In short, he must deal with the call in a professional manner, one which not only resolves the problem at hand, but, in addition, increases goodwill and reduces callbacks. The structured learning training program described in this chapter is designed to train officers for these several goals.

As we have described in the preceding chapter, structured learning consists of four components, each of which is a well-established training procedure. These procedures are modeling, role playing, social reinforcement and transfer training.

In each training session, a group of eight to twelve trainees are:

1. Played a brief videotape or shown a live demonstration depicting specific skill behaviors shown to be helpful in dealing with common problems of police work (modeling).
2. Given extensive opportunity, encouragement and training to behaviorally rehearse, or practice, the effective behaviors they have heard (role playing).
3. Provided corrective feedback and approval or praise as their role playing of the behaviors becomes more and more similar to the tape or live model's behavior (social reinforcement).
4. And, most important: Asked to participate in each of these procedures in such a way that transfer of the newly-learned behaviors from the training setting to the trainee's real-life setting will be highly likely (transfer training).

Before describing the procedures involved in organizing and actually running structured learning sessions in further detail, we wish to mention briefly what structured learning is *not.* First, it is important to stress that the skill behaviors (learning points) portrayed by the taped or live model should not be viewed as the one and only way to enact the skill effectively. The goal of structured learning training is to help build a flexible selection of effective and satisfying behaviors which the officer can adjust to the demands of the situation. Thus, we urge you to consider the recommended skill behaviors as good examples (as they indeed have been shown to be), but not as the only way to effectively perform the skill involved.

A second caution, for those of you using the structured learning modeling tapes, is that these are not instructional tapes in the usual sense. An instructional tape is most typically played to an audience which passively listens to it, and then, at some later date, is supposed to do what was played. Such passive learning is not likely to be enduring learning.[1] Thus, the structured learning modeling tapes should not be played alone, i.e., without role playing and feedback following them. We have demonstrated experimentally that all four components of this training approach are necessary and sufficient for enduring behavior change, and these results should be reflected in the use of these materials and procedures.

---

[1] It is for this same reason, i.e., the inadequacy of passive learning, that we have avoided, here, relying heavily on lectures.

Finally, structured learning is not an approach which can be used effectively by all possible trainers. Later in this chapter we will describe in detail the knowledge, skills and sensitivities which a trainer must possess to be effective with this approach.

ORGANIZING THE STRUCTURED LEARNING GROUP

Selection of Trainees

Each structured learning group should consist of trainees who clearly need training in whatever skill is going to be taught. If possible, trainees should also be grouped according to the *degree* of their deficiency in the given skill; otherwise, they will progress at different rates. Some may become bored while others are still struggling to learn simple skills, and yet other trainees may become resistant. The optimal sized group for effective structured learning sessions should consist of eight to twelve trainees plus two trainers.

For both learning and transfer to occur, each trainee must have ample opportunity to practice what he has seen modeled, receive feedback from other group members and the trainers, and discuss his attempts to apply on the job what he has learned in the training sessions. Yet, each typical session should not exceed two hours in length, since structured learning is intensive, and trainees' efficiency of learning often diminishes beyond this span. A group size of eight to twelve, therefore, is optimal in that it permits the specific training tasks to be accomplished within the allotted time period.

Number, Length and Spacing of Sessions

The structured learning procedures typically constitute a training program which requires using a number of different modeling tapes, or live skill demonstrations, depending on which skills are being taught. For each skill we have sought to teach, we have developed a different live or taped modeling display. The specific behaviors which make up the skill are concretely demonstrated in each display. The order in which the modeling tapes or live skill demonstrations are utilized should:

1. Give trainees a sense of making progress in skill mastery (thus, the easier skills should come first).

2. Provide them (in each session) with useful knowledge which can be applied in real life (between sessions) with at least some of the persons with whom they usually interact.

It is most desirable that training occur at a rate of approximately two meetings per week. *Spacing is crucial.* Most trainees in all skill training programs learn well in the training setting. Most, however, fail to transfer this learning to where it counts — at work in the community. As you will see below, structured learning includes special procedures which maximize the likelihood of transfer of training, including between-sessions field work. These periods of trying out the newly learned skills in real-life situations must be well-spaced. We have found two or three meetings per week optimal.

TRAINERS

The role-playing and feedback activities which make up most of each structured learning session are a series of "action-reaction" sequences in which effective skill behaviors are first rehearsed (role playing), and then critiqued (feedback). As such, the trainer must both lead and observe. We have found that one trainer is very hard pressed to do both of these tasks well at the same time, and, thus, recommend strongly that each session be led by a team of two trainers.

Their group leadership skills, interpersonal sensitivity, enthusiasm, and a favorable relationship between them are the qualities which appear crucial to the success of training. They must also possess in-depth knowledge of good police procedure, rules and regulations. If they have had considerable road experience, they will be much more credible to the trainees. In addition to these considerations, structured learning trainers must be especially proficient in two types of skills.

The first might best be described as *General Trainer Skills,* i.e., those skills required for success in almost any training effort. These include:

1. Oral communication and group discussion leadership.
2. Flexibility and capacity for resourcefulness.
3. Physical energy.
4. Ability to work under pressure.

5. Empathic ability.
6. Listening skill.
7. Broad knowledge of human behavior.

The second type of requisite skills are *Specific Trainer Skills*, i.e., those relevant to structured learning in particular. These include:

1. In depth knowledge of structured learning, its background, procedures and goals.
2. How to orient both trainees and supporting staff to structured learning.
3. How to initiate and sustain role playing.
4. Ability to present material in concrete, behavioral form.
5. How to reduce and "turn around" trainee resistance.
6. Procedures for providing corrective feedback.
7. Group management skills, e.g., building cohesiveness, "clique-busting," etc.

For both trainer selection and development purposes, we have found it most desirable to have potential trainers participate, as if they were actual trainees, in a series of structured learning sessions. After this experience, we have had them co-lead a series of sessions with an experienced trainer. In doing so, we have shown them how to conduct such sessions, given them several opportunities to practice what they have seen, and provided them with feedback regarding their performance. In effect, we have used structured learning to teach structured learning.

THE STRUCTURED LEARNING SESSIONS

The Setting

One major principle for encouraging transfer from the training setting to the real-life setting is the rule of identical elements. This rule states that the more similar the two settings (i.e., the greater number of identical physical and social qualities they share), the greater the transfer. Training in a fancy office or at a country retreat may be great fun, but it results in minimal transfer of training. We urge you to conduct structured learning in the same general setting as the real-life environment of most participating trainees, and to construct and furnish the training setting to resemble or simulate the likely application setting as much as possible.

You should arrange the training room to make the structured learning procedures easier. A horseshoe layout in which chairs are arranged in the shape of a U is one good example of such a helpful arrangement. Two additional chairs should be placed up front for the role players. Behind and to the side of the role players, on the right, place a chalkboard. Write the learning points (specific skill behaviors) you're working with at that time, on the board. You should avoid a conference or seminar arrangement of furniture in which trainees sit around a table, as you will reduce the action-oriented quality of training and make realistic role playing more difficult.

As we will note, the trainees who play the role of responding officers in the problem situation are required to follow and enact the skill's learning points in their role playing. This is a key procedure in structured learning. If possible, other parts of this same room should be furnished (depending on the particular skill being taught) to resemble (at least in rudimentary form) a patrol car, a kitchen, a bar, a store counter, an office, or other relevant application settings. In designing the setting, it's also important to keep in mind the trainees' descriptions of where and with whom they have difficulty performing the skill. When no appropriate furniture or materials are available to "set the scene," you can use substitute or even imaginary props.

Open the session by having trainers introduce themselves. Then have each trainee do likewise. Be sure that every trainee has the opportunity to tell the group something about his or her background and training goals. After the initial warm-up period, introduce the program by providing trainees with a brief description of its rationale, training procedures, skill targets and so forth. Typically, in our introduction, we also cover such topics as the importance of skill in working with a very wide variety of people for effective and satisfying police work; the value of skill knowledge and flexibility to the trainee himself; and the manner in which training focuses on altering specific behaviors, and not on attitude change. You'll probably want to do this too. Next, spend some time discussing these introductory points. After this, you can begin the actual training.

Modeling

The training begins by playing the first modeling tape. To ease trainees into structured learning, use tapes of relatively simple skill behaviors (learning points) in your first session. Such content is not likely to arouse anxiety as it consists of specific skill behaviors or learning points which are not difficult to enact.

All modeling tapes begin with a narrator setting the scene and stating the tape's learning points. Sets of actors — one or two of whom are in the role the trainees are to adopt during later role playing (responding officers) — portray a series of vignettes in which each learning point is clearly enacted in sequence. The narrator then returns (on the tape), reviews the vignettes, restates the learning points, and urges their continued use. In our view, this sequence — narrator's introduction, modeling scenes, narrator's summary — constitutes the minimum requirement for a satisfactory modeling tape. In greater detail, we recommend the following format for effective modeling tapes:

I.   Narrator's Introduction

    1. Introduction of self.
      a. Name and title.
      b. High status position, e.g., Chief of Police.

    2. Introduction of skill.
      a. Name of skill, e.g., Calming the Situation.
      b. General (descriptive) definition.
      c. Operational (learning points) definition.

    3. Incentive statement. How and why skill-presence may be rewarding.

    4. Discrimination statement. Examples of skill-absence, and how and why skill-absence may be unrewarding.

    5. Repeat statement of learning points, and request for attention to what follows.

II.   Modeling Displays

A number of vignettes of the learning point behaviors are presented, each vignette portraying the complete set of learning points which make up the given skill. A variety of actors (models) and situations are used. Model characteristics (age, sex, apparent socio-economic level, etc.) are similar to typical trainee characteristics. Situation characteristics should also reflect common, real-life environments.

The displays portray overt model behaviors, as well as ideational and self-instructional (what one says to oneself) learning points. Models are provided social reward or reinforcement for enacting the skill. The vignettes are presented in order of increasing complexity.

III. Narrator's Summary

1. Repeat statement of learning points.

2. Description of rewards to both models and actual trainees for skill usage.

3. Urging of observers to enact the learning points in the structured learning training session which follows, and, subsequently, in their real-life environment.

It will often be the case that because of lack of appropriate equipment, materials, or personnel, the use of modeling videotapes will not be possible. However, you can still carry out an effective structured learning program to teach crisis intervention skills. Under these circumstances we recommend that you use live modeling of the crisis intervention skills discussed in this manual. Trainers, and experienced officers selected by them, can play the police and citizen roles which make up each skill demonstration.

It is very important that you carefully prepare each live modeling presentation. Scripts must be carefully planned, thoroughly rehearsed, and skillfully enacted before the group. All of the learning points of a given skill must be clearly portrayed, and in the proper order. The content of each live modeling demonstration must credibly present a crisis call in a totally realistic manner, or its effectiveness will be minimal. In all, if adequately planned and portrayed, live modeling can be every bit as effective as using videotapes.

Extensive experience with structured learning training of crisis intervention skills in the Syracuse Police Department reveals that skilled and effective crisis intervention by police officers consists of the four separate skills examined in detail in Chapter 2:

I. Observing and Protecting against Threats to Your Safety.

II. Calming the Situation.

III. Gathering Relevant Information.

IV. Taking Appropriate Action.

In the Syracuse program, each of these four skills was broken down into the behaviors (learning points) which made up the skill. In essence, if an officer carries out the set of learning points, he has carried out the skill. The learning points for each skill are:

I.   **Observing and Protecting against Threats to Your Safety**
     1. Consider your prior experience on similar calls.
     2. Anticipate that the unexpected may actually happen.
     3. Form a tentative plan of action.

II. **Calming the Situation**
     1. Observe and neutralize threats to your safety.
     2. Create a first impression of non-hostile authority.
     3. Calm the emotional citizen.

III. **Gathering Relevant Information**
     1. Explain to the citizen what you want him to discuss with you and why.
     2. Interview the citizen so as to gain details of the crisis as clearly as possible.
     3. Show that you understand the citizen's statements and give accurate answers to his questions.
     4. Revise your plan of action if appropriate.

IV. **Taking Appropriate Action**
     1. Carefully explain your plan of action to the citizen.
     2. Check that the citizen understands and agrees with your plan of action.
     3. Carry out your plan of action.

In the Syracuse training program, the trainers introduced and summarized the modeling tapes[2] with the following statements:

Introduction to Observing and Protecting against Threats to Your Safety. Today you are going to view a videotape which will demonstrate a skill which is very important in effectively dealing with police calls. This skill is observing and protecting against threats to your safety. When you are dispatched to a

---

[2] With very minor changes, you can use these same modeling display introductions to introduce live modeling of the four skills.

call you must prepare yourself in order to respond quickly and effectively. In the good examples which you will now observe, the officer does three basic things:

1. Considers his prior experience in similar situations.
2. Anticipates that the unexpected may actually happen.
3. Forms a tentative plan of action.

When the officer does these three things, he is better prepared to approach the situation with confidence in his professional skill, and to take the most effective action. If the officer does not consider his prior experience in similar situations, anticipate that the unexpected may actually happen, and form a tentative plan of action, he will not be well-prepared. The situation may take him by surprise, the outcome being ineffective use of his skill, or worse, personal injury.

You will now see and listen to examples of officers preparing to respond to a call by observing and protecting against threats to their safety. The people on these tapes are not professional actors, but are police officers in the Syracuse Police Department. We would like you to learn these three steps in order to get the benefits of being an effective police officer, so please pay close attention.

(Play tapes.)

You have just seen and heard what experienced police officers do and think as they prepare to respond to a call. In observing and protecting against threats to their safety, they: first, consider their prior experience in similar situations; second, anticipate that the unexpected may actually happen; and third, form a tentative plan of action. In order to help you refine these skills, the training staff will now direct your attention to specific features of these skills and prepare you for rehearsing this technique.[3]

Introduction to Calming the Situation. You will recall that the behavioral skill illustrated on the first videotape was observing and protecting against threats to your safety. The tape

---

[3] To aid in the role playing of this skill, the trainer "dispatched" the calls appearing in Appendix I, and the trainees were required to respond in terms of the learning points.

you will now see illustrates appropriate police behavior in a second phase of the intervention: calming the situation. The specific learning points which make up skillfully calming the situation include:

1. Observe and neutralize threats to your safety.
2. Create a first impression of non-hostile authority.
3. Calm the emotional citizen.

How successful you will be in resolving the conflict or crisis depends heavily on your actions soon after you arrive at the crisis scene. The first step in the actual intervention is calming the situation or restoring order. Before intervening can begin to get at the source of the problem, the situation must be calm. Note carefully the techniques used by the officers in combining officer authority with professional procedure and personal concern, to effectively calm the situation.[4]

Introduction to Gathering Relevant Information. In the previous tapes, you have seen police officers preparing to respond to a call, and beginning to intervene by calming the situation. Specific techniques have varied, and situations have required different actions. We have emphasized flexibility. Today you will observe the skills used by the officers in carrying out the necessary investigation. Again, we will emphasize techniques and the types of helpful responses exhibited by the officers. Specifically, the major points illustrated in this tape on gathering relevant information are:

1. Explain to the citizen what you want him to discuss with you and why.

2. Interview the citizen so as to gain details of the crisis as clearly as possible.

3. Show that you understand the citizen's statements and give accurate answers to his questions.

4. Revise your plan of action if appropriate.

---

[4] To aid in the role playing of this skill, you should provide trainees with the descriptions of the several specific methods recommended in Chapter 2 for calming the emotional citizen.

The success of your crisis intervention depends heavily on how well you have carried out your investigation. Good investigation is at the heart of police procedure. A police officer always takes action, and that action depends on what he sees, hears, and believes about the situation. This phase of the training will help you in developing your skills as an investigator.[5]

Introduction to Taking Appropriate Action. The skills we have worked with up to this point have all been geared toward handling the crisis situation in such a way that it ends with appropriate police action being taken. If the officer protects himself, calms the persons involved, and determines in sufficient detail what is happening, he will be in a position to deal with the crisis in a professional, competent manner. Today you will observe the specific skills involved in taking such appropriate action.[6] These skills are:

1. Carefully explain your plan of action to the citizen.

2. Check that the citizen understands and agrees with your plan of action.

3. Carry out your plan of action.

Following these steps will enable you to make optimal use of the information you have gathered, and bring the crisis to an appropriate resolution.

Role Playing

A spontaneous discussion will almost invariably follow the playing of a modeling tape or the live demonstration of a skill. Trainees

---

[5] To aid in the role playing of this skill, you should provide trainees with a form such as the Syracuse Police Department's Family Crisis Intervention Report (see Appendix II), which contains the topics usefully covered in the officer's investigation. You also need to teach trainees *how* to obtain crisis-relevant information. To accomplish this, you should make them familiar (by means of role playing) with the several interviewing techniques recommended in Chapter 2.

[6] To aid trainees in role playing this skill, you should provide a description of the specific courses of action recommended for crisis situations in Chapter 2.

will comment on the learning points, the actors, and very often, on how the situation or skill problem shown occurs in their own work. At this point in time, you should divide the trainees into groups of four trainees each, and instruct them to prepare for role playing. This preparation is designed to make the role playing, which follows viewing of the modeling tapes, as realistic as possible.

The purpose of structured learning is not practice of exercises handed down by someone else, not re-handling old crisis calls but, instead, *behavioral rehearsal;* that is, practice for crisis events and situations which the trainee is actually likely to face. Each group of four trainees is instructed to develop a crisis event (planning the specific roles of disputants, victim, offender, or other citizen), and enact this crisis as realistically as possible to two other officer-trainees who have been instructed to deal with the crisis by following the learning points illustrated on the modeling tapes or live demonstrations. The specific instructions you give to the trainees preparing the crisis enactment follow.

Role-Playing Instructions

Your task during this preparation period will be to design a skit in which a dispute occurs (the disputants' relationship will be designated by a trainer). Afterwards, the skit will be performed with members of your group portraying the disputants, while one or more members of another group portray a police officer intervening in that dispute. Representatives of your group will then participate in the critique which follows the skit.

The skit will require careful preparation for effectiveness as a learning/teaching method. We suggest you cover the following steps:

1. Talk about cases you've known that fit the designation; and, select one that can be effectively portrayed, and that promises to be a good learning vehicle for the audience.
2. Discuss the personalities and situations involved.
3. Select group members to portray the roles.
4. Help the actors become familiar with their roles, with what they will say and do before the "police" arrive.

5. Help the actors practice and become "natural" in their roles. Discourage overacting! It is *essential* that after the police arrive, your actors react naturally to what the "police" do, and not according to some script. Remember, when your skit is presented, after the intervening officer(s) arrive, the actors should respond to the officer(s) as they think their characters would respond.

As noted earlier, the crisis situation is acted out, and two other trainees are chosen to serve as the responding officers. Their task is to handle the crisis effectively — by following the skill's learning points. All other trainees in the larger group serve as observers, whose later feedback is designed to be of use to the two responding officers.

Before the given role play actually begins, you should deliver the following instructions:

1. *To the two trainees responding to the call (responders):* In responding to the call you are about to hear, follow and enact the learning points. Do not leave any out, and follow them in the proper sequence.

2. *To the trainees enacting the crisis situation (disputants):* React as naturally as possible to the behavior of the responding officers. Within the one limitation of not endangering anyone's physical safety, it is important that your reactions to the responding officers be as real-life as possible.

3. *To all other trainees (observers):* Carefully observe how well the responding officers follow the learning points, and take notes on this for later discussion and feedback.

One of the trainers then instructs the role players to begin. It is your main responsibility at this point to be sure responders keep role playing, and that they try to follow the learning points while doing so. If they "break role," and begin making comments or explaining background events, etc., you should firmly instruct them to resume their roles. One trainer should position himself near the chalkboard and point to each learning point in turn, as the role play unfolds, being sure none are missed or enacted out of order. If either responder feels the role play is not progressing well and wishes to start it over, this is appropriate. Do not permit interruptions of any kind from the group until the role play is completed.

The role playing should be continued until all the skits have been presented and all trainees (responders) have had an opportunity to participate, even if the same skill and learning points must be carried over to a second or third session. Note that while the framework (learning points) of each role play in the series remains the same, the actual content should change from role play to role play. It is crises as they actually occur, or could occur, which should be the content of the given role play. When completed, each trainee should be better armed to act appropriately in the given reality situations.

We would like to point out a few further procedural matters relevant to role playing, as each will serve to increase its effectiveness. Role reversal is often a useful role-play procedure. An officer role playing a crisis problem may have a difficult time perceiving the disputants' viewpoint, and vice versa. Having them exchange roles and resume the role playing can be most helpful in this regard.

At times, it may be worthwhile for the trainer to assume the disputant role, in an effort to expose trainees to the handling of types of reactions not otherwise role played during the session. It is here that your flexibility and creativity will certainly be called upon. Finally, role playing at times may become *too* realistic and the possibility of physical injury to one of the participants may appear likely. You should carry a whistle to use in the event that it becomes necessary to stop the role playing immediately.

Corrective Feedback/Social Reinforcement

After completing each role play, you should have a brief feedback period. The goals of this activity are to let the responders know how well they "stayed with" the learning points, or in what ways they departed from them. It also lets them know the psychological impact of their enactment on the disputants, and encourages them to try out the role-play behaviors in real life. To implement this feedback process we suggest you follow a sequence of eliciting comments from:

1. *The role-play disputants,* i.e., "How did the officers (responders) make you feel?" "What are you likely to do now?"
2. *The observing trainees,* i.e., "How well were the learning points followed?" "What *specific* behaviors did you like or dislike?"
3. *The trainers,* who comment, in particular, on how well the learning points were followed; and who provide social reinforcement

(praise, approval, encouragement) for close following. To be most effective, reinforcement provided by the trainers should be offered in accordance with the following rules:

a. Provide reinforcement *immediately* after role plays which follow the learning points.
b. Provide reinforcement *only* after role plays which follow the learning points.
c. Vary the specific content of the reinforcements offered.
d. Provide enough role-playing activity for each group member to have sufficient opportunity to be reinforced.
e. Provide reinforcement in an amount consistent with the quality of the given role play.
f. Provide no reinforcement when the role play departs significantly from the learning points (except for "trying" in the first session or two).
g. In later sessions, space out the reinforcement you provide so that not every good role play is reinforced.

4. *The role-play responders themselves,* who comment on their own enactment, on the comments of others, and on their specific expectations regarding how, when, and with whom they might attempt the learning points in their work environment.

In all these critiques, it is crucial that you maintain the behavioral focus of structured learning. Comments must point to the presence or absence of specific, concrete behaviors, and not take the form of general evaluative comments or broad generalities. Feedback, of course, may be positive or negative in content. At minimum, you can praise a "poor" performance (major departures from the learning points) as "a good try" at the same time you criticize its real faults.

If at all possible you should give trainees who fail to follow the relevant learning points in their role play, the opportunity to re-role play these same learning points after they've received corrective feedback. At times, as a further feedback procedure, we have audiotaped or videotaped entire role plays. The "actors" are often too busy "doing" to reflect on their own behavior. Giving them later opportunities to observe themselves on tape can be an effective aid to learning.

Since a prime goal of structured learning is skill flexibility, a role-play trainee who departs markedly from the learning points may not necessarily be "wrong." That is, what he does may, in fact, "work" in some situations. Trainers should stress that it is an effective *"alternative"* they are trying to teach, and that the trainee would do well to have it in his repertoire (collection) of skill behaviors — available to use when it is appropriate.

As a final feedback step, after all role playing and discussion of it is completed, you should replay the modeling tape, or repeat the live demonstration of the particular skill. This step, in a sense, summarizes the session and leaves trainees with a final overview of the learning points.

Transfer Training

The prime purpose of several aspects of the training sessions described above is to enhance the likelihood that learning in the training setting will transfer to the trainee's actual work environment. Making sure that the trainees in the disputant role create a crisis event which is as realistic as possible (both in terms of their own behavior and the physical setting and props of the role play) is one example of an aid to transfer.

Another is to try to have the two trainees who are in the responder role for a given skit, be two officers who actually work together on the road. Sheer practice is another means which increases the chances that what the officers learn in training will be used in the community. Such practice of the learning points of a skill occurs by not only serving as a responder, but also when the trainee serves as either a disputant or an observer.

But even when a training program contains considerable realistic practice, some trainees will still be unable to bridge the gap between performing in the training center and applying the skill at work. The Syracuse Program sought to resolve this problem by having one of the program trainers ride with each trainee a few hours each week to give further real-life instruction and feedback. While such a procedure may be expensive in time and manpower, a training program which fails to transfer is, quite obviously, much more expensive.

Transfer of training is also a function of the trainee's motivation. "Learning" concerns the question: *Can* he do it? "Performance" is a matter of: *Will* he do it? Trainees will perform as trained if, and only if, they have genuine and active environmental support. Stated simply, new behaviors persist if they are rewarded; diminish if they are ignored or actively challenged. Obviously, therefore, you should not undertake a structured learning program (or any training program) unless you can realistically expect some appreciable level of environmental support from your command and other supervisory personnel.

Resistance and Resistance Reduction

As happens in all training approaches, a minority of the trainees who take part in structured learning may resist. In one or more of a variety of ways, they may seek to block or avoid trainer efforts to conduct the session as we have defined it throughout this manual. They may argue about the accuracy or relevance of the content of the modeling tape or live demonstration; they may claim that the absence of danger during role playing makes it so different from real life that it is useless; they may show boredom, disinterest and unconcern. In all, we have identified fifteen different ways in which resistance may occur. We have listed the types of resistance in Table 1, and briefly mentioned the general approaches to reducing such resistance which we have found useful. In Table 2, we have more fully identified several means for dealing effectively with trainee resistance.

TABLE 1. Types of Trainee Resistance

I. **Active Resistance to Participation**
    1. Participation, but not as instructed
    2. Refusal to role play
    3. Lateness
    4. Cutting

Reduce this resistance by: a) encouraging empathically, b) reducing threat, c) instructing.

II. **Inappropriate Behavior**
    1. Can't remember
    2. Inattention
    3. Excessive restlessness

Reduce this resistance by: a) simplifying, b) terminating responses, c) instructing.

III. **Inactivity**
    1. Apathy

2. Minimal participation
3. Minimal ability to understand

Reduce this resistance by: a) reducing threat, b) eliciting responses, c) instructing.

IV. **Hyperactivity**
1. Interrupts
2. Monopolizes
3. Trainer's helper
4. Jumping out of role
5. Digresses

Reduce this resistance by: a) encouraging empathically, b) terminating responses, c) reducing threat.

TABLE 2. Methods for Reducing Trainee Resistance

I. **Simplification Methods**
1. Reinforce minimal trainee accomplishment.
2. Shorten the role play.
3. Have the trainee read a script portraying the learning points.
4. Have the trainee play a passive role (or even a non-speaking role) in role playing.
5. Have trainee follow one learning point.
6. Have trainer "feed" sentences to the trainee.

II. **Threat Reduction Methods**
1. Use live modeling of responder role by the trainer.
2. Reassure trainee.
3. Clarify any aspects of the trainee's task which are still unclear.

III. **Elicitation of Responses Methods**
1. Call for volunteers.
2. Introduce topics for discussion.
3. Ask specific trainee to participate, preferably choosing someone who has made eye contact with the leader.

IV. **Termination of Responses Methods**
1. Interrupt ongoing behavior.
2. Extinguish through inattention to trainee behavior.
3. Back off contact and get others to participate.
4. Urge trainee to get back on correct track.

V. **Instruction Methods**
1. Coach and prompt.
2. Instruct in specific procedures and applications.

VI. **Empathic Encouragement Method (Six Steps)**
1. Offer the resistant trainee the opportunity to explain in greater detail his reluctance to role play, and listen non-defensively.
2. Clearly express your understanding of the resistant trainee's feelings.
3. If appropriate, respond that the trainee's view is a viable alternative.
4. Present your own view in greater detail, with both supporting reasons and probable outcomes.
5. Express the appropriateness of delaying a resolution of the trainer-trainee difference.
6. Urge the trainee to tentatively try to role play the given learning points.

EVALUATION OF STRUCTURED LEARNING FOR POLICE TRAINING

During 1974, the Syracuse Police Department developed and implemented an LEAA-funded training program aimed at teaching proficiency in crisis intervention skills to Syracuse police.[7] In all, 225 officers participated. The project was conducted using the Structured Learning Training procedures and materials described in this chapter. This "classroom" phase of the training effort was supplemented by six weeks of field training in which a trainer rode with each officer-trainee on an intermittent basis, and sought to make the transfer of classroom skill learning to community application easier.

A major attempt was made to examine the effectiveness of the Syracuse training program. First, at the completion of the classroom phase, the field training, and an eight-month follow-up, an opinion questionnaire was given to all participating officers. Results were

---

[7]Dr. Clive Davis, Psychology Department, Syracuse University, shared co-responsibility for the direction of this training project, with Sgt. Philip Monti, and bore primary responsibility for its evaluation.

clear cut. Almost all of the officers felt that they had greater understanding of crisis intervention procedures, felt they were more effective in response to crisis calls, and would recommend the program to
others.

While such positive opinion ratings provide useful information,
what the officers actually *do* is certainly more powerful evidence
than what they *say* or *feel*. To obtain such realistic data, participating
officers were presented with simulated crises during training; and,
after training, their intervention behaviors on actual crisis calls were
observed. The evaluation report states:

> Each available videotaped recording of the simulated interventions (79
> interventions conducted by 157 officers) that occurred during the final
> day of training was evaluated by the judges. A sample of 47 actual in-
> terventions conducted by 91 different officers during regular patrol duty
> were also evaluated by the police judges. These evaluations were based
> on first-hand observation of the interventions. The results were consis-
> tent. In both the simulated and actual interventions the majority of offi-
> cers evidenced effective use of good intervention techniques . . . (pp. 174-
> 175).

Thus, both the officers themselves, and objective observers of their
actual crisis intervention behaviors, indicate that the training program is a success.

But what of the "consumers," the citizens involved in the crisis
calls? A sampling group of 57 citizens involved in crisis calls were
contacted and interviewed about their treatment by the police. Again,
results were clearly positive. Citizens reported that responding officers were courteous, polite, wanting to be of assistance, listening to
both sides, trying to get at the cause of the problem, and, in the large
majority of instances, successful. These citizen reports, therefore,
combine with the police and observer data to confirm the value of
Structured Learning for purposes of teaching crisis intervention skills
to police.

IV

Appendices

Calls "Dispatched" for Role Playing

Family Crisis Intervention Report

Suggested Readings

I Calls "Dispatched" for Role Playing

Calls "Dispatched" for Role Playing

1. Sig. 76-0300: Repeat call — man a heavy drinker — young kids in the family — apartment house.

2. Sig. 80-1630: Brighton Avenue — exit of 81 — rush hour traffic.

3. Sig. 81-2330: Bar — man with a gun — you will be the first car on the scene.

4. Sig. 85-1515: Apparent 3141, Marshall Street — nude male walking in the middle of the street.

5. Sig. 76-2030: Middle-class neighborhood — first call to this house, phoned in by neighbor — woman screaming for man not to beat her anymore.

6. Sig. 87-1530: Holiday Inn downtown — woman passed out at the bar.

7. Sig. 77-2305: Teenagers drinking in park after high school football game.

8. Sig. 82-0045: Grocery store Valley Plaza Code 4 — appears to be more than one person in store according to citizen who phoned in.

9. Sig. 85-1210:   Child not home from school for lunch — not at school either — not on route to and from school — mother very upset.

10. Sig. 76-2100:   Regular repeat call — heavy drinkers both — he's a fighter.

11. Sig. 78-1530:   Possible attempted suicide — female 16 years old.

12. Sig. 85-1930:   Landlord/tenant dispute in the street — crowd gathering — you are first to arrive.

Family Crisis Intervention Report

1. Reporting Officer _____

2. D.R. No. (Or date and 72, 73 times) _____

3. Assisting Officers (a) _____
                     (b) _____

4. Names, Addresses, etc., of principal disputants. (**Important** — If missing, note reason.)

   A. _____
       name   *address*   *age* *sex* *phone*

   B. _____
       name   *address*   *age* *sex* *phone*

   C. _____
       name   *address*   *age* *sex* *phone*

   D. _____
       name   *address*   *age* *sex* *phone*

   List below the ages and sex of any others (including children) present.

   _____

5. What was the reason for the call for police? (e.g., fight, noise, etc.)

   _____

6. When you arrived the situation was: 1   2   3   4   5
                                   violent   *agitated*   *calm*

7. Were any of the disputants **impaired** by alcohol or drugs? _____ Yes _____ No
   If yes, which parties? ___ A ___ B ___ C ___ D (Letters refer to persons named above.)

8. Was there a weapon involved? _____ Yes _____ No If yes, specify: _____

9. Describe the disputants' behavior. (Use A, B, C, D as named above for each party.)

1	2	3	4	5	6	7
very resistant			*indifferent*		*very cooperative*	

10. What was the basic problem underlying the crisis? (Describe in detail.)

    _____

    _____

    _____

11. Was this the first call to the police about the situation? _____ Yes _____ No
    _____ Don't know

12. Describe the specific actions which you took. (Use back if more space is needed.)

    _____

    _____

    _____

    Final Action Codes   /   /   /   Was a referral made? _____ Yes _____ No
    If yes, to whom? _____ Volunteer _____
    Other (specify) _____ Was the agency call made in your presence? _____ Yes _____ No   By you? _____ Yes _____ No

13. How satisfied do you think the parties were with your assistance? (Use A, B, C, D as above.)

1	2	3	4	5	6	7
very unsatisfied			*neutral*		*very satisfied*	

14. What do you think was the effect of the intervention?
    _____ Dispute not resolved, likely to recur
    _____ Dispute not resolved, but disputants cooled off
    _____ Dispute resolved, some understanding on both sides
    _____ Dispute resolved, issue settled

III   Suggested Readings

Suggested Readings

You may wish to seek additional knowledge about one or more of the main topics we've covered in this text. The books listed below are all recommended readings for this purpose.

Structured Learning

Goldstein, A.P. *Structured learning therapy.* New York: Academic Press, 1973.

Goldstein, A.P., & Goedhart, A. The use of structured learning for empathy enhancement in paraprofessional psychotherapist training. *Journal of Community Psychology,* 1973, 1, 168-173.

Goldstein, A.P., & Sorcher, M. *Changing supervisor behavior.* New York: Pergamon Press, 1973.

Goldstein, A.P., & Monti, P.J. *Crisis intervention manual for police.* Syracuse, N.Y.: Syracuse Police Department, 1976.

Goldstein, A.P., Sprafkin, R., & Gershaw, N.J. *Skill training for community living: Applying structured learning therapy.* New York: Pergamon Press, 1976.

Crisis Intervention — General Readings

Lieb, J., Lipsitch, S.I., & Slaby, A.E. *The crisis team.* New York: Harper & Row, 1973.

McGee, R.K. *Crisis intervention in the community.* Baltimore: University Park Press, 1974.

Parad, H.J. (Ed.). *Crisis intervention: Selected readings.* New York: Family Service Association, 1965.

Specter, G.A., & Claiborn, W.L. *Crisis intervention.* New York: Behavioral Publications, 1973.

Crisis Intervention — Police

Brooks, P.R. *Officer down, code three.* Schiller Park, Ill.: Motorola Teleprograms, 1975.

Cohen, R., Sprafkin, R.P., Oglesby, S., & Claiborn, W. *Working with police agencies.* New York: Behavioral Publications, 1976.

Cromwell, P.F., & Keefer, G. *Police-community relations.* St. Paul: West Publishing Co., 1973.

Kobetz, R.W. *Crisis intervention and the police: Selected readings.* Gaithersburg, Md.: International Association of Chiefs of Police, 1974.

Schonborn, K. *Dealing with violence.* Springfield, Ill.: Charles C. Thomas, 1975.

Westley, W.A. *Violence and the police.* Cambridge, Mass.: MIT Press, 1970.

Family Disputes

Blood, R.O., & Wolfe, D.M. *Husbands and wives.* New York: The Free Press, 1969.

Plattner, P. *Conflict and understanding in marriage.* Richmond, Va.: John Knox Press, 1970.

Steinmetz, S.K., & Straus, M.A. *Violence in the family.* New York: Dodd, Mead & Co., 1974.

Abnormal Behavior

Cammer, L. *Up from depression.* New York: Simon & Schuster, 1969.

Johnson, R.N. *Aggression in man and animals.* Philadelphia: W.B. Saunders, 1972.

Suinn, R.M. *Fundamentals of behavior pathology.* New York: John Wiley, 1970.

Interviewing

Banaka, W.H. *Training in depth interviewing.* New York: Harper & Row, 1971.

Fenlason, A.F., Ferguson, G.B., & Abrahamson, A.E. *Essentials in interviewing: For the interviewer offering professional services.* New York: Harper & Row, 1962.

Rich, J. *Interviewing children and adolescents.* London: Macmillan, 1968.

Negotiation

Nierenberg, G.I. *The art of negotiating.* New York: Cornerstone Library, 1968.

Counseling

Brammer, L.M. *The helping relationship: Process and skills.* Englewood Cliffs, N.J.: Prentice-Hall, 1973.

Carkhuff, R.R. *Helping and human relations.* New York: Holt, Rinehart & Winston, 1969.

Kanfer, F.K., & Goldstein, A.P. *Helping people change.* New York: Pergamon Press, 1975.

TITLES IN THE PERGAMON GENERAL PSYCHOLOGY SERIES (Continued)